VICKIE HOWELL

Wee Garter Stitch

VICKIE HOWELL

Wee Garter Stitch

MUST-HAVE KNITS FOR
MODERN BABIES & TODDLERS

sixth&springbooks | NEW YORK

 **sixth&springbooks** | 161 Avenue of the Americas, New York, NY 10013   sixthandspringbooks.com

Library of Congress Cataloging-in-Publication Data

Howell, Vickie, author.
 Wee garter stitch : must-have knits for modern babies and toddlers / by Vickie Howell. -- First edition.
    pages cm
 Includes index.
 ISBN 978-1-942021-92-6 (pbk.)
1. Infants' clothing. 2. Knitting--Patterns. I. Title.
 TT640.H69 2016
 746.43'2--dc23

Manufactured in China

1 3 5 7 9 10 8 6 4 2

FIRST EDITION

Executive Editor
Carla Scott

Editor
Carol Sulcoski

Editorial Assistant
Jacob Seifert

Patterns Editors
Renee Lorion and
Lori Steinberg

Technical Editor
Loretta Dachman

Art Director
Diane Lamphron

Fashion Stylist
Joanna Radow

Assistant Stylist
Emily Whitted

Photography
Dave Campbell (Techniques)
Dan Howell (Models)
Marcus Tullis (Still-life)

Vice President/Editorial Director
Trisha Malcolm

Publisher
Carrie Kilmer

Production Manager
David Joinnides

President
Art Joinnides

Chairman
Jay Stein

For Yoshi, Rocco,
Sailor, and Mako,
the wee (and not-so-wee) babies
whose sweet faces and cool style served
as inspiration for much of this book.

Contents

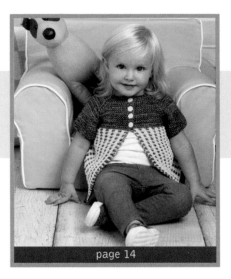
page 14

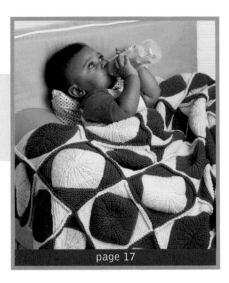
page 17

page 26

page 28

page 35

page 38

page 20

page 22

page 24

page 30

page 40

page 32

page 42

page 44

page 46

page 56

page 58

page 48

page 50

page 53

page 60

page 63

page 66

page 68

page 71

I was a little late to the knitting party—comparatively, anyway.

I started sewing and crocheting when I was eight years old; embroidering and other crafts came years before that. For whatever reason, though, knitting just didn't stick. Not that is, until many years later, when I was pregnant with my second child.

As for many new knitters, the lure of making baby booties and sweet little sweaters hit me hardest when I had someone in mind to wear them. When I picked up my sticks for the first time as an adult, knitting was still widely considered a grandmother's craft (not that there's anything wrong with that), and certainly not one that could interest young mothers, movie execs, rock stars, or feminists. After leaving a promising career path in the entertainment industry to be a stay-at-home mom, I began to wonder: was picking up knitting just another form of rebellion against the "modern woman" I strived to become?

I didn't know. What I was sure of, however, was that the little boy in my belly would look adorable in the knit bunny hat featured in the (now-defunct) *Martha Stewart Baby Magazine*. After a trip to Southern California's La Knitterie Parisenne—where women from all walks of life gathered to create, surrounded by the most beautiful yarns I'd ever seen—I was hooked. For me, it was time to knit. That day, my misconceptions melted away, and a new passion was born. Six months later, so was my beautiful boy, Tristan.

The upcoming birth of a child often inspires people to venture into the knitting world for the first time, led by the smallest of hands. Maybe that's why, for me, baby garments are gateways to possibility. They represent new life, fresh ideas, attainable creation. And one of the first stitches a new knitter learns is garter stitch.

Garter stitch is considered the perfect stitch for new knitters because it's basic—you simply knit every row. But that very simplicity often causes garter stitch to be dismissed as boring. In my humble opinion, garter stitch is one of the coolest stitches of the bunch. When paired with crisp palettes or watery pools of color and simple shapes, garter stitch's clean ridges and textural bumps create a truly modern-looking piece. Nurture the stitch with advanced skills like short rows, stranded colorwork, or lace motifs, and that simple stitch evolves into something unexpected.

Wee Garter Stitch was written as an ode to how simple beginnings can often lead to smart results. Cool and classic can also be creative and (in the case of the projects in this book) cuddly. So pick up those sticks and get ready to play. Together, we(e) garter stitch!

xx,
VICKIE

The Projects

Mini Mosaic Cardi

MOSAIC STITCHES in neon are set off by a neutral garter-stitch bodice in this sweet, short-sleeved sweater. Pair it with a sundress or a wee pair of jeans and t-shirt; either way your bébé will look brilliant!

SIZES
Instructions are written for size 6 months (12 months, 2T). Shown in size 12 months.

MEASUREMENTS
CHEST:
22 (23, 26)"/56 (58.5, 66)cm
LENGTH:
11 (12, 14)"/28 (30.5, 35.5)cm
UPPER ARM:
7½ (8, 9½)"/19 (20.5, 24)cm

MATERIALS
■ 1 (1, 2) 3½oz/100g skeins (each 270yd/247m) of Madeleine Tosh *Tosh Sport* (superwash merino wool) each in Rainwater (A) and Edison Bulb (B) **2**

■ One size 5 (3.75mm) circular needle, 24"/60cm long, *or size to obtain gauge*

■ One set (5) size 5 (3.75mm) double-pointed needles (dpns)

■ Scrap yarn

■ Four ½"/13cm buttons

■ Sewing needle and thread

■ Stitch markers

GAUGES
■ 24 sts and 48 rows to 4"/10cm over mosaic pat using size 5 (3.75mm) needle.
■ 21 sts and 42 rows to 4"/10cm over garter st using size 5 (3.75mm) needle. *Take time to check your gauges.*

MOSAIC PATTERN
(multiple of 4 sts, plus 2)
Rows 1 and 2 With B, knit.
Row 3 (RS) With A, k2, *sl 2 purlwise wyib, k2; rep from * to end.

Row 4 With A, k2, *sl 2 purlwise wyif, k2; rep from * to end.
Rep rows 1–4 for mosaic pat.

BUTTONHOLE ROW
RS row K2, (yo) twice, k to last 2 sts, (yo) twice, k2. Yo's are not included in st counts.
In foll row, knit, dropping yo's without working them.

NOTES
1) Cardigan is worked in one piece from the lower edge up.
2) Cardigan is worked in rows. Circular needle is used to accommodate large number of sts. Do *not* join.

BODY
With circular needle and A, cast on 130 (134, 154) sts.
Knit 4 rows.
Work in mosaic pat until piece measures 7¾ (8½, 10)"/19.5 (21.5, 25.5)cm from beg, end with a row 4.

DIVIDE FOR FRONT AND BACK
K28 (29, 33), bind off next 5 sts, knit until there are 64 (66, 78) sts on needle after armhole, bind off next 5 sts, k to end—120 (124, 144) sts.
Set piece aside.

SLEEVES (MAKE 2)
With dpns and A, cast on 40 (42, 50) sts. Join, taking care not to twist sts, pm for beg of rnd.
Work 16 rnds in garter st (k 1 rnd, p 1 rnd).
Place on scrap yarn and set aside.

14

YOKE

Joining row (RS) With A, k to armhole, pm, k35 (37, 45) sleeve sts from scrap yarn, leaving 5 sts on scrap yarn, pm, k64 (66, 78) back sts, pm, k35 (37, 45) sleeve sts from scrap yarn, leaving 5 sts on scrap yarn, pm, k to end—190 (198, 234) sts.

Next (set-up) row (WS) K to first marker, dec'ing 4 sts evenly across left front, sl marker, k35 (37, 45) sleeve sts, sl marker, k to next marker, dec'ing 8 (6, 10) sts evenly across back, sl marker, k35 (37, 45) sleeve sts, sl marker, k to end, dec'ing 4 sts evenly across right front—174 (184, 216) sts, 24 (25, 29) sts for each front, 56 (60, 68) sts for back.

Next (dec) row (RS) [K to 2 sts before next marker, k2tog tbl, sl marker, k2tog] 4 times, k to end—8 sts dec'd.

Cont in garter stitch, rep dec row every other row 14 (15, 18) times more, AT SAME TIME, work buttonhole every 8th (8th, 10th) row 4 times—54 (56, 64) sts.

Knit 1 WS row.

NECKBAND

Knit 2 rows.
Bind off.

FINISHING

Sew open sleeve sts to bound-off underarm sts.
Sew buttons to left front correspond to buttonholes. ■

10¼ (10¾, 12)"

11 (12, 14)"

7½ (8, 9½)"

3¼ (3½, 4)"

7¾ (8½, 10)"

BODY

22 (23, 26)"

Round Peg Blanket

SHORT-ROW CIRCLES surrounded by garter corners create a geometric snuggle-scape. This blanket is soft enough for little kid's naptime, but mod enough for big kid to take to college.

MEASUREMENTS
Approx 39 x 39"/99 x 99cm

MATERIALS
■ 5 3½oz/100g skeins (each 218yd/200m) of Plymouth Yarns *Select Worsted Merino Superwash* (superwash merino wool) each in #0041 Lagoon (A) and #0001 Natural (B) ④

■ One pair size 8 (5mm) needles *or size to obtain gauge*

■ One set (5) size 8 (5mm) double-pointed needles (dpns)

■ Size H/8 (5mm) crochet hook

■ Scrap yarn

■ Four stitch markers

GAUGES
■ 20 sts and 40 rows to 4"/10cm over garter st using size 8 (5mm) needles.
■ 1 square = 7 x 7"/18 x 18cm.
Take time to check your gauges.

BLOCK A (MAKE 18)
CENTER
With A, crochet hook, and straight needles, cast on 12 sts, using provisional cast-on method (see page 78).
Knit 1 row.
*Short row 1 (RS) K11, sl 1, bring yarn to front, return sl st to LH needle, turn (sl st is wrapped), k to end on WS.

Short row 2 (RS) K8, sl 1, bring yarn to front, return sl st to LH needle, turn, k to end on WS.
Short row 3 (RS) K6, sl 1, bring yarn to front, return sl st to LH needle, turn, k to end on WS.
Short row 4 (RS) K4, sl 1, bring yarn to front, return sl st to LH needle, turn, k to end on WS.

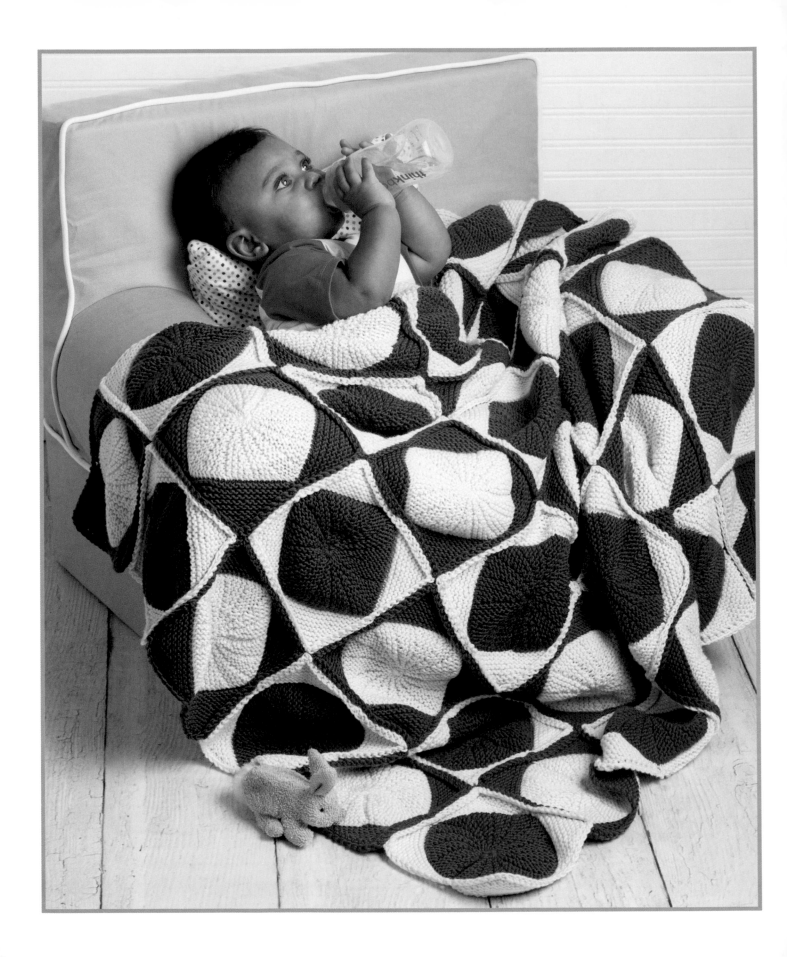

Your big kid wants in on the blanket action? Make 24 of each block for lapghan size!

Short row 5 (RS) K2, sl 1, bring yarn to front, return sl st to LH needle, turn, k to end on WS.
Rep from * 16 times more to complete circle.

Carefully remove scrap yarn chain from provisional cast-on and place sts on spare needle. Join cast-on row to final row using Purl 3-needle bind-off method (see page 90).

EDGING

Note This edging is worked in four parts using a series of short-rows. Each corner is formed where 2 dpns meet, and the markers denote the centers of the flat edges of the square. The entire edging is worked in rounds, but each corner is worked in rows.

*With B and 1 dpn, using purl bumps as a guide, pick up and k 20 sts evenly (placing a stitch marker after 10 sts) over 1 quarter of the circle, rep from * for rem 3 quarters with 3 separate dpns—80 sts.

Corner 1 (dpns 1 and 2)

Note Corner is worked on sts between 2 markers at a time.

Row 1 (RS) K to 1 st before marker; sl 1, bring yarn to front, return sl st to LH needle, turn.

Row 2 (WS) K to 1 st before marker; sl 1, bring yarn to front, return sl st to LH needle, turn.

Rows 3 and 4 K to 2 sts before marker; sl 1, bring yarn to front, return sl st to LH needle, turn.

Rows 5 and 6 K to 3 sts before marker; sl 1, bring yarn to front, return sl st to LH needle, turn.

Rows 7 and 8 K to 4 sts before marker; sl 1, bring yarn to front, return sl st to LH needle, turn.

Rows 9 and 10 K to 5 sts before marker; sl 1, bring yarn to front, return sl st to LH needle, turn.

Rows 11 and 12 K to 6 sts before marker; sl 1, bring yarn to front, return sl st to LH needle, turn.

Rows 13 and 14 K to 7 sts before marker; sl 1, bring yarn to front, return sl st to LH needle, turn.

Rows 15 and 16 K to 8 sts before marker; sl 1, bring yarn to front, return sl st to LH needle, turn.

Rows 17 and 18 K to 9 sts before marker; sl 1, sl 1, bring yarn to front, return sl st to LH needle, turn.
One corner is complete.

Corner 2

Next row (RS) K to 1 st before next marker and rep rows 1–18.
Cont in this manner until all 4 corners are complete. K to end of rnd (next marker).
Bind off as foll:
K2, insert LH needle into front legs of 2 sts on RH needle and k2tog through the back loops; *k1, insert LH needle into front legs of 2 sts on RH needle and k2tog through the back loops; rep from * until all sts are bound off.

BLOCK B (MAKE 18)
Work as for block A, using B for center and A for edging.

FINISHING
Block each square to measurements (*this is important!*). Sew squares together in a 6 x 6 checkerboard pattern using photo as a guide as foll: with wrong side of two squares together, working 1 row inside of outer edges, sew adjoining pieces together. The seamed edges will curl to the outside. ∎

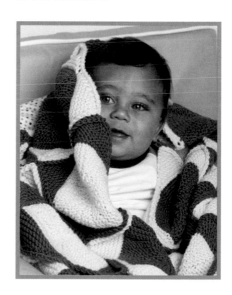

Signature Slouchy Beanie

LIGHTWEIGHT SLOUCHY BEANIES ARE QUICK TO KNIT, cool to wear, and easy to embellish with an initial, appliqué, or a bow. Give 'em to all the babies in your life!

SIZE
Instructions are written in one size that stretches to fit up to 16"/40.5cm head circumference.

MEASUREMENTS
BRIM CIRCUMFERENCE (UNSTRETCHED):
12"/30.5cm
LENGTH:
6½"/16.5cm

MATERIALS
■ 1 2.4oz/70g skein (each 282yd/258m) of Bernat *Cotton-ish by Vickie Howell* (cotton/acrylic) in each in #16208585628 Cotton Harvest (A) and #16208585044 Grey T-Shirt (B) **③**

■ Small amount in #16208585734 Turquoise Terry Cloth (C)

■ One set (5) size 5 (3.75mm) double-pointed needles (dpns) *or size to obtain gauge*

■ Stitch marker

■ Tapestry needle

GAUGE
■ 24 sts and 40 rnds to 4"/10cm over garter st using size 5 (3.75mm) needles.
Take time to check your gauge.

GARTER STRIPE PATTERN
Rnd 1 With B, knit.
Rnd 2 With B, purl.
Rnd 3 With A, knit.
Rnd 4 With A, purl.
Rep rnds 1–4 for garter stripe pat.

HAT
With A, cast on 72 sts. Join, being careful not to twists sts, and pm for beg of rnd.
Rnds 1–5 *K2, p2; rep from * around.

BEG GARTER STRIPE PAT
Rep rnds 1–4 of garter stripe pat until piece measures 5½"/14cm from beg. Cut B and cont with A to end.

SHAPE CROWN
Rnd 1 [K4, k2tog] 12 times around—60 sts.
Rnds 2, 4, 6, 8 and 10 Purl.
Rnd 3 [K3, k2tog] 12 times around—48 sts.
Rnd 5 [K2, k2tog] 12 times around—36 sts.
Rnd 7 [K1, k2tog] 12 times around—24 sts.
Rnd 9 [K1, k2tog] 8 times around—16 sts.
Rnd 11 [K2tog] 8 times around—8 sts.
Cut yarn, leaving a 6"/15cm tail. Thread tail through rem sts to close.

FINISHING
BOW
With C, cast on 10 sts. Work in garter st (k every row) until piece measures 3¾"/9.5cm from beg. Bind off. Wind a length of C several times, tightly, around center of piece to form bow. Fasten to hat with center just above ribbed brim and ends even with lower edge of hat. ■

Simple Stripey Socks

TINY TOES IN SOFT STRIPES are sure to melt even the hardest of hearts. Hidden benefit: garter bumps give extra padding for those teeny tootsies!

SIZE
To fit sizes Newborn (6–12 months). Shown in sizes Newborn and 6–12 months.

MEASUREMENTS
CIRCUMFERENCE:
Approx 4 (4½)"/10 (11)cm
LENGTH FROM HEEL TO TOE:
3 (4)"/7.5 (10)cm
LENGTH FROM BOTTOM OF HEEL TO TOP OF LEG:
4 (4 ½)"/10 (11)cm

MATERIALS
■ 1 2.4oz /70g skein (each 166yd/152m) of Patons *Kroy Socks* (washable wool/nylon) in #24345555245 Spring Leaf Stripes (newborn) or #24345555048 Grey Brown Marl (6–12 months) **①**

■ One set (4) size 3 (3.25mm) double-pointed needles (dpns) *or size to obtain gauge*

■ Stitch marker

■ Stitch holder

GAUGE
■ 24 sts and 48 rows to 4"/10cm over garter stitch using size 3 (3.25mm) needles.
Take time to check your gauge.

SOCKS
CUFF
Cast on 24 (28) sts. Divide sts evenly on three dpns. Join, being careful not to twist sts, and pm for beg of rnd.
Next rnd *K1, p1; rep from * around for k1, p1 rib.
Work 3 rnds more in rib.
Work in garter st (k 1 rnd, p 1 rnd) until piece measures 2½"/6.5 cm from edge.

HEEL FLAP
Note Heel flap is worked in rows on 12 (14) sts only.
Place 12 (14) sts on 1 dpn for heel, keeping rem sts on hold for instep.
Row 1 (RS) *Sl 1, k1; rep to end.
Row 2 Sl 1, k to end.
Rep rows 1–2 twelve (fourteen) times more, then rep row 1 once.

TURN HEEL
Row 1 (WS) Sl 1, k6 (7), k2tog, k1, turn.
Row 2 Sl 1, k1 (2), ssk, k1, turn.
Row 3 Sl 1, k2 (3), k2tog, k1, turn.
Row 4 Sl 1, k3 (4), ssk, k to end—8 (10) sts.

GUSSET
Rnd 1 Place half of the heel sts on a free dpn (Needle 1), with same dpn, pick up and k 7 (8) sts along first side of heel; place instep sts on Needle 2, k12 (14); Needle 3, pick up and k 7 (8) sts along 2nd side of heel, k rem heel flap sts—11 (13) sts each on Needles 1 and 3, 12 (14) sts on Needle 2—34 (40) sts in rnd.

Rnd 2 Purl.
Rnd 3 Needle 1, K to last 3 sts, k2tog, k1; Needle 2, Knit; Needle 3, K1, ssk, k to end—2 sts dec'd.
Rnd 4 Purl.
Rep rnds 3–4 four (five) times more—24 (28) sts.
Work even in garter st until foot measures 2½ (3)"/6.5 (7.5cm), end with a purl rnd.

SHAPE TOE
Arrange the sts so that there are 12 (14) on Needle 2, and 6 (7) each on Needles 1 and 3.
Rnd 1 Needle 1, K to last 3 sts, k2tog, k1; Needle 2, K1, ssk, k to last 3 sts, k2tog, k1; Needle 3, K1, ssk, k to end—4 sts dec'd.
Rnd 2 Purl.
Rep rnds 1–2 twice more—12 (16) sts rem.

FINISHING
Divide sts evenly on 2 needles, graft using garter Kitchener stitch (see pages 88–89). ■

Paper Chain Garland

SIMPLE STRIPS of garter stitch come to life in an old-school homage to childhood.

MEASUREMENTS
13-loop chain is approx 40"/101.5cm long

MATERIALS
■ 1 2.4oz/70g skein (each 282yd/258m) of Bernat *Cotton-ish by Vickie Howell* (cotton/acrylic) each in pop colors: #16208585734 Turquoise Terry Cloth (A), #16208585628 Cotton Harvest (B), and #16208585020 Lemon Twill (C)
OR neutral colors: #16208585044 Grey T-shirt (A), #16208585008 Cotton Ball (B), and #16208585012 Coffee Filter (C) ③

■ One pair size 5 (3.75mm) needles *or size to obtain gauge*

GAUGE
24 sts and 40 rows to 4"/10cm over garter st using size 5 (3.75mm) needles.
Take time to check your gauge.

STRIP (MAKE 5 IN A, 4 EACH IN B AND C)
Cast on 12 sts.
Work in garter st (k every row) until piece measures 12"/30.5cm from beg. Bind off, leaving a long tail for sewing.

FINISHING
Sew cast-on edge to bound-off edge of first A strip, forming a loop. Place B strip through loop and sew ends tog. Cont in A, B, C color sequence, join rem strips, end with A. ■

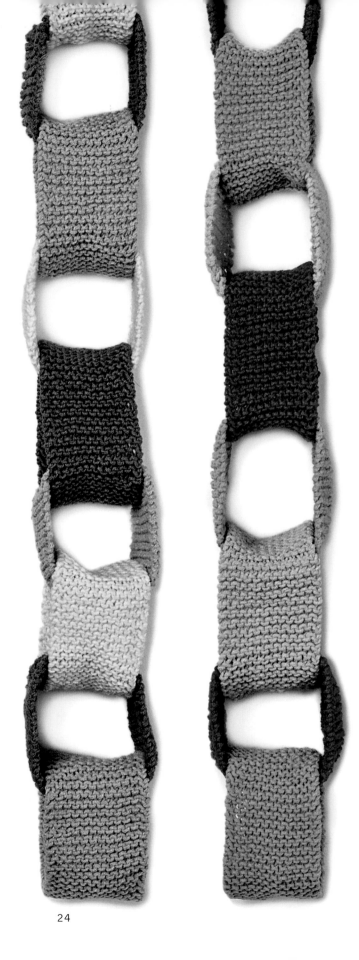

Toasty Toboggan

TEXTURE TURNS TOASTY in this ready-for-winter hat, worked in wide garter rib with cozy earflaps. A giant neon pompom adds a touch of whimsy to the cap's traditional shape.

■■■■□

SIZE
Instructions are written for size 12 months.

MEASUREMENTS
HEAD CIRCUMFERENCE: 16"/40cm
LENGTH: 6½"/16.5cm

MATERIALS
■ 2 3½oz/100g skeins (each 120yd/110m) of Bernat *Alpaca* (acrylic/alpaca) in #16109393007 Natural ⑤

■ One size 10 (6mm) circular needle, 16"/40cm long, *or size to obtain gauge*

■ One set (4) size 10 (6mm) double-pointed needles (dpns)

■ 1 Bernat Faux Fur Pompom in #16700101223 Bright Green

■ Stitch marker

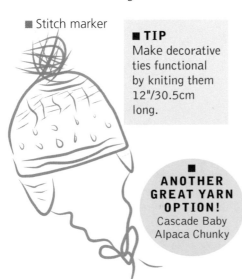

■ TIP
Make decorative ties functional by knitting them 12"/30.5cm long.

■ ANOTHER GREAT YARN OPTION!
Cascade Baby Alpaca Chunky

STITCH GLOSSARY
2-st RT K 2nd st on LH needle without slipping st off needle, k first st and let both sts slip to RH needle.

GAUGE
14 sts and 24 rnds to 4"/10cm over pattern st using size 10 (6mm) needle.
Take time to check your gauge.

PATTERN STITCH
(multiple of 4 sts)
Rnd 1 *K2, 2-st RT; rep from * around.
Rnd 2 *P2, 2-st RT; rep from * around.
Rep rnds 1 and 2 for pat st.

HAT
Cast on 56 sts. Join, being careful not to twist sts, and place marker for beg of rnd.
Work 6 rnds in garter st (k 1 rnd, p 1 rnd).

BEG PAT ST
Rep rnds 1 and 2 of pat st until piece measures 4½"/11.5cm from beg, end with a rnd 2.

SHAPE CROWN
Note Change to dpns, dividing evenly on 3 needles, when sts no longer fit comfortably on circular needle.
Rnd 1 (dec) [K6, k2tog] 7 times around—49 sts.
Rnd 2 and all even numbered rnds Purl.
Rnd 3 (dec) [K5, k2tog] 7 times around—42 sts.
Rnd 5 (dec) [K4, k2tog] 7 times around—35 sts.

Rnd 7 (dec) [K3, k2tog] 7 times around—28 sts.
Rnd 9 (dec) [K2, k2tog] 7 times around—21 sts.
Rnd 11 (dec) [K1, k2tog] 7 times around—14 sts.
Rnd 13 (dec) [K2tog] 7 times around—7 sts.
Cut yarn, leaving a tail 6"/15cm long. Thread tail through rem sts to close.

FINISHING
EAR FLAPS
With RS facing and dpns, using beg of rnd as center back of hat, pick up and k 12 sts along lower edge at side of hat.
Knit 3 rows.
Next (dec) row (RS) K2tog tbl, k to last 2 sts, k2tog—10 sts.
Knit 3 rows.
Next (dec) row (RS) K2tog tbl, k to last 2 sts, k2tog—2 sts dec'd.
Cont in garter st (k every row) and rep dec row every other row twice more—4 sts. Do *not* turn.

TIE
Row 1 Slide sts to opposite end of dpn to work next row from RS, pull yarn tightly across back of work and k4.
Row 2 Slide sts to opposite end of dpn to work next row from RS, pull yarn tightly across back of work and p4.
Rep rows 1 and 2 until tie measures 4"/10cm. Bind off and cut yarn, leaving a tail 1½"/4cm long.
Rep on opposite side for 2nd earflap. Use the tail ends to tie.

Sew pompom to top of hat. ■

Fox Lovie Blanket

LITTLE HANDS LOVE A LOVIE—LIKE THIS FRIENDLY FOX, who is part pal, part security blanket. It's designed to be hugged, dragged, and kept with its wee owner whenever he or she needs it.

MEASUREMENTS
Approx 22 x 19"/56 x 48cm

MATERIALS
■ 3 1¾oz /50g skeins (each 103yd/94m) of Classic Elite Yarns *Verde Collection Chesapeake* (cotton/wool) in #5906 Tigerlily (A) 🄸

■ Small amount of #5938 Bracken (C)

■ 3 1¾oz/50g skeins (each 115yd/105m) of Rowan *Softknit Cotton* (cotton/polyamide) in #588 White (B) 🄸

■ One pair size 7 (4.5mm) needles *or size to obtain gauge*

■ One set (5) size 6 (4mm) double-pointed needles (dpns)

■ Stitch markers

■ Small amount of polyester stuffing

■ 1 safety eye

■ Tapestry needle

GAUGE
■ 23 sts and 30 rows to 4"/10cm over pat st using size 7 (4.5mm) needles. *Take time to check your gauge.*

PATTERN STITCH
(multiple of 18 sts plus 2)
Rows 1 and 2 Knit.
Row 3 K1, *[k2tog] 3 times, [yo, k1] 6 times, [k2tog] 3 times; rep from * to last st, k1.
Row 4 Knit.
Rep rows 1–4 for pat st.

NOTE
Place stitch markers between each pattern repeat.

BLANKET
With A and larger needles, cast on 128 sts.
[With A work 16 rows in pat. Cut A. With B, work 16 rows in pat . Cut B.] 4 times. With A, work 16 rows in pat st. Bind off.

HEAD
With A and dpns, cast on 20 sts. Divide sts evenly on 4 dpns. Join, being careful not to twist sts, and place marker (pm) for beg of rnd. Work 4 rnds in garter stitch (k 1 rnd, p 1 rnd).

Next (inc) rnd *K1, kfb; rep from * around—30 sts.
Work 5 rnds even.
Next (inc) rnd *K2, kfb; rep from * around—40 sts.
Work 3 rnds even.
Next (inc) rnd *K3, kfb; rep from * around—50 sts.
Work 3 rnds even.
Next (inc) rnd: *K4, kfb; rep from * around—60 sts.
Cont even in garter st until piece measures 2½"/6.5cm from beg.

SHAPE TOP
Next (dec) rnd *K4, k2tog; rep from * around—50 sts.
Work 3 rnds even.
Next (dec) rnd *K3, k2tog; rep from * around—40 sts.
Work 3 rnds even.
Next (dec) rnd *K2, k2tog; rep from * around—30 sts.
Work 3 rnds even.
Next (dec) rnd *K1, k2tog; rep from * around—20 sts.
Next rnd Purl.
Next (dec) rnd *K2tog; rep from * around.
Rep last 2 rnds—5 sts.
Cut yarn leaving a long tail, set aside.

EARS (MAKE 2)
With 2 dpns and A, cast on 12 sts. Knit 2 rows.
Next (dec) row K1, k2tog tbl, k to last 3 sts, k2tog, k1—2 sts dec'd.
Next row Knit.
Rep last 2 rows once more—8 sts. Cut A; join C.
Rep last 2 rows twice more—4 sts.
Next (dec) row K1, k2tog, k1—3 sts.
Knit 1 row.
Next row SK2P. Fasten off.

FACE
With larger needles and B, cast on 20 sts.
Work 8 rows in pat st. Cut B. With A, work 8 rows in pat st. Bind off.

FINISHING
Sew ears and face to head, using photo as guide.
With C and tapestry needle, embroider eyelids and lashes on white portion of face.
Attach safety eye for nose at the tip of white portion of face.
Stuff head. Thread tail through rem sts to close. Sew head to center of blanket on RS with face facing bound-off edge. ■

Horseplay Zebra Mat

SHORT-ROW "STRIPES" AND A CUSHY, CHENILLE-FEEL YARN create this zebra-inspired play mat. Knit one of these for your wee one, and watch tummy time take a turn for the wild.

MEASUREMENTS
Approx 35 x 35"/89 x 89cm, not including head and hooves

MATERIALS
■ 2 5.3oz /150g skeins (each 108yd/98m) of Bernat *Blanket* (polyester) in #1612000006 Vintage White (A) **6**

■ 1 skein in #16120000044 Dark Gray (B)

■ One pair size 11 (8mm) needles *or size to obtain gauge*

■ One size 13 (9mm) needle for binding off only

GAUGE
■ 7 sts and 16 rows to 4"/10cm over garter stitch using size 11 (8mm) needles.
Take time to check your gauge.

LEFT-SLANTING WEDGE
Knit 2 rows.
Short row 1 (RS) K56, sl 1, bring yarn to front, return sl st to LH needle, turn (last st is wrapped), k to end.
Short row 2 (RS) K to 4 sts before wrapped st, bring yarn to front, return sl st to LH needle, turn, k to end.
Rep short row 2 until 4 sts rem, end with a WS row.

RIGHT-SLANTING WEDGE
Next row (RS) Knit over all sts.
Short row 1 (WS) K56, sl 1, bring yarn to front, sl st back to LH needle, turn, k to end.

Short row 2 (RS) K to 4 sts before wrapped st, bring yarn to front, return sl st to LH needle, turn, k to end.
Rep short row 2 until 4 sts rem, end with a RS row. Knit 1 row over all sts.

STRIPE PAT
In garter st, 2 rows A, 2 rows B. Rep these 4 rows for stripe pat.

BLANKET
With A, cast on 60 sts.
Note Do *not* carry unused color up side. Cut and join at each color change.
Work left-slanting wedge with A.
Work right-slanting wedge with B.
*Work 12 rows in garter st with A.
Work left-slanting wedge with B.
Work 12 rows in garter st with A.
Work right-slanting wedge with B.
Rep from * once more.
Work 12 rows in garter st with A.
Work left-slanting wedge with B.
Work right-slanting wedge with A.
With A, knit 2 rows.
Bind off loosely using larger needle.

HOOF (MAKE 4)
Note Twist colors while carrying up the side for a decorative look.
With A, cast on 9 sts.
Knit 2 rows. Join B.
Next (inc) row (RS) K1, kfb, k to last 2 sts, kfb, k1—2 sts inc'd.
Cont in stripe pat as established, rep inc row every other row twice more—15 sts.
With A, knit 3 rows. Bind off.

HEAD
With A, cast on 10 sts.
Work 4 rows in stripe pat.
Next (inc) row (RS) With A, k1, kfb, k to last 2 sts, kfb, k1—2 sts inc'd.
Cont in stripe pat, rep inc row every 4th row 4 times more, end with an A stripe—20 sts.
With A, knit 1 row. Bind off.

EAR (MAKE 2)
With B, cast on 6 sts. Knit 6 rows.
Next (dec) row (RS) K2tog tbl, k2, k2tog. Knit 1 row.
Next (dec) row (RS) K2tog tbl, k2tog, pass 2nd st over first st. Fasten off.

FINISHING
Sew ears to head. Sew head to center of bound-off edge of mat. Sew hooves to the 4 corners, using photo as a guide. Weave in ends.

TAIL
Cut 2 strands each of A and B, approx 32"/81cm long. Holding strands tog, fold in half to form loop. With crochet hook, pull loop through a st in center of cast-on edge. Draw ends of strands through loop and tighten. Trim ends even. ■

Best Dress-ed

THIS DRESS PAIRS SWEETNESS WITH STRENGTH to suit a modern mama's idea of dress-up. Worked from the top down in one piece, just keep on knitting if baby keeps growing before you've finished!

SIZES
Instructions are written for size 6 months (12 months, 2T). Shown in size 6 months.

MEASUREMENTS
CHEST:
17½ (18½, 20½)"/44.5 (47, 52)cm
LENGTH:
13½ (14½, 15½)"/34.5 (37, 39.5)cm
UPPER ARM:
7 (7½, 8)"/18 (19, 20.5)cm

MATERIALS
■ 2 (3, 3) 1¾oz/50g hanks (each 181yd/166m) of Quince & Co. *Chickadee* (wool) in Dogwood (A) 🄻

■ 1 hank each in Bosc (B), Belize (C), and Storm (D)

■ One each sizes 4 and 5 (3.5 and 3.75mm) circular needle, 16"/40cm long, *or size to obtain gauge.*

■ Round, removable stitch markers

■ Small velvet bow

■ Hook and eye

■ Sewing needle and thread

■ Scrap yarn

GAUGE
23 sts and 46 rows to 4"/10cm over garter st using larger needle.
Take time to check your gauge.

NOTES
1) Dress is worked flat from cast-on edge to bodice, then joined for knitting in the round.
2) Because garter stitch is knit both flat and in the round, be sure to swatch both ways to make sure your gauge matches.

DRESS
With larger needles and A, cast on 59 (63, 67) sts. Do *not* join. Working back and forth in rows, work as foll:
Knit 3 rows.
Set-up row (WS) K10 (11, 12) for right back, place marker (pm), k9 for sleeve, pm, k21 (23, 25) for front, pm, k9 for sleeve, pm, k10 (11, 12) for left back.
Next (inc) row (RS) [K to marker, yo, sl marker, k1, yo] 4 times, k to end—8 sts inc'd.
Cont in garter st (k every row) and rep inc row every other row 11 (12, 13) times more—155 (167, 179) sts.
Knit 1 row.

BODICE
Join and pm for beg of rnd.
Next (inc) rnd [K to marker, yo, sl marker, k1, yo] 4 times, k to end—8 sts inc'd.
Purl 1 rnd.
Cont in garter st (k 1 rnd, p 1 rnd) and rep inc rnd every other rnd twice more—179 (191, 203) sts.

DIVIDE FOR FRONT AND BACK
Next rnd K25 (27, 29), place next 39 (41, 43) sts on scrap yarn for sleeve, k51 (55, 59), place next 39 (41, 43) sts on scrap yarn for 2nd sleeve, k25 (27, 29)—101 (109, 117) sts in rnd for body. Cont in garter st, work until bodice measures 6 (6½, 7)"/15 (16.5, 18)cm from beg.
Change to smaller needle.

Next rnd Knit, dec 5 sts evenly around—96 (104, 112) sts.
Next 8 rnds *K2, p2; rep from * around. Pm to mark last rnd. Change to larger needles.
Next (inc) rnd Knit, inc 32 sts evenly around—128 (136, 144) sts. Work even in garter st until piece measures 2½ (3, 3½)"/6.5 (7.5, 9)cm from marker.

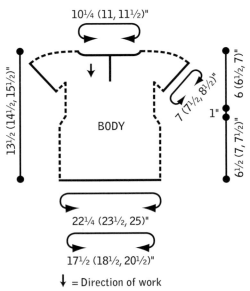

10¼ (11, 11½)"

13½ (14½, 15½)"

7 (7½, 8½)"

6 (6½, 7)"

1"

6½ (7, 7½)"

BODY

22¼ (23½, 25)"

17½ (18½, 20½)"

↓ = Direction of work

Make an adorable peplum top by skipping the charted portion!

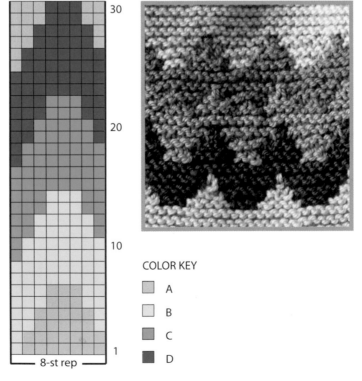

BEGIN CHART

Rnd 1 Work 8-st chart rep 16 (17, 18) times around.
Cont to work chart in this manner until rnd 30 of chart is complete. With A, work 6 rnds in garter stitch.
Next (eyelet) rnd *Yo, k2tog; rep from * around.
Next rnd Purl.
Work 2 rnds in garter st. Bind off.

SLEEVES (MAKE 2)

With RS facing, A and dpns, k39 (41, 43) sleeve sts from scrap yarn, and pick up and k 2 (3, 3) sts along underarm. Join and pm for beg of rnd—41 (44, 46) sts. Work 2 rnds in garter stitch. Join B. Work 2 rnds in garter stitch. Cut B.
Next rnd With A, knit, dec 1 (0, 0) st—40 (44, 46) sts.
Next 3 rnds: *K1, p1; rep from * around.
Bind off in rib.
Rep for 2nd sleeve.

FINISHING

Sew bow to front neckline, using photo as guide. Sew hook and eye to back neck opening. ■

30

20

10

1

8-st rep

COLOR KEY

A

B

C

D

Cable Baby Cardi

SHAKE UP THE CLASSIC CABLED CARDIGAN by opting for a garter stitch background and slip-stitch cables. Bonus: this cardi's knit in one piece with minimal finishing, perfect for busy moms.

SIZES
Instructions are written for size 6 months (12 months, 2T). Shown in size 6 months.

MEASUREMENTS
CHEST:
18 (21, 24)"/45.5 (53.5, 61)cm
LENGTH:
10 (11, 12)"/25.5 (28, 30.5)cm
UPPER ARM:
7¾ (8¼, 8¾)"/19.5 (21, 22)cm

MATERIALS
■ 2 (2, 3) 3oz/85g skeins (each 167yd/153m) of Bernat *Sheep-ish by Vickie Howell* (acrylic/wool) in #16416900019 Navy(ish) ④

■ One size 8 (5mm) circular needle, 24"/60cm long, *or size to obtain gauge*

■ One set (5) of size 8 (5mm) double-pointed needles (dpns)

■ Stitch markers

■ Scrap yarn

■ 7 (8, 9) ½"/13mm buttons

■ Cable needle (cn)

■ Sewing needle and thread

■ ANOTHER GREAT YARN OPTION!
Classic Elite Minnow Merino By Jill Eaton

GAUGE
16 sts and 32 rows to 4"/10cm over garter st using size 8 (5mm) needle. *Take time to check your gauge.*

STITCH GLOSSARY
6-st sl st LC Sl 3 sts to cn and hold to *front*, k2, sl 1; sl 1, k2 from cn. (see page 86)

CABLE PANEL
(over 6 sts)
Rows 1, 3 and 5 (RS) Sl 1, k4, sl 1.
Rows 2, 4 and 6 P1, k4, p1.
Row 7 6-st sl st LC.
Row 8 Rep row 2.
Rep rows 1–8 for cable panel.

NOTES
1. Cardigan is worked in one piece from the neck down.
2. Cardigan is worked in rows. Circular needle is used to accommodate large number of sts. Do *not* join.
3. Stitches are slipped purlwise wyib.

NECK
Cast on 34 (42, 50) sts.
Row 1 (RS) *K2, p2; rep from *, end k2.
K the knit sts and p the purl sts for k2, p2 rib for 3 rows more.

SHAPE YOKE
Set-up row (RS) K6 (8, 10) for right front, place marker (pm), k5 for 1st sleeve, pm, k12 (16, 20) for back, pm, k5 for 2nd sleeve, pm, k6 (8, 10) for left front.
Next row Knit.
Next (inc) row (RS) [K to 1 st before marker, yo, k1, sl marker, k1, yo] 4 times, k to end—8 sts inc'd.
Cont in garter st and rep inc row every other row 3 times more—66

(74, 82) sts.

BEGIN CABLE PANELS AND RAGLAN SHAPING
Next (inc) row K3, pm, work 6 sts foll row 1 of cable panel, pm, *k to 1 st before marker, yo, k1, sl marker, k1, yo; rep from * 3 times more, k to last 10 sts, pm, work 6 sts foll row 1 of cable panel, pm, k4—8 sts inc'd. Cont in garter st , working cable panel as established, and rep inc row every 4th row 7 (8, 9) times more—130 (146, 162) sts.

BODY
Next row (RS) Cont in garter st and cable panels to 1st marker, place 29 (31, 33) sts on scrap yarn for sleeve, remove 1st and 2nd markers, k to 3rd marker, place 29 (31, 33) sts on scrap yarn for sleeve, remove 3rd and 4th markers, work to end—72 (84, 96)sts for body. Place markers in each end of this row, do not slip these markers.
Work even until body measures 2½ (3, 3½)"/6.5 (7.5, 9)cm from markers, end with a WS row and dec 2 sts evenly over last row—70 (82, 94) sts.
Next row (RS) *K2, p2; rep from * to end, k2.
Work in k2, p2 rib for 2"/5cm. Bind off loosely in rib.

SLEEVES (MAKE 2)
Note Sleeves are worked in rounds using dpns.

Place sleeve sts evenly on dpns, picking up 1 st at each side of underarm—31 (33, 35) sts. Pm for beg of rnd.
Work 6 rnds in garter st (k 1 rnd, p 1 rnd), slipping marker every rnd.
Next (dec) rnd K2tog, k to last 3 sts, ssk, k1—2 sts dec'd.
Rep dec rnd every 6th (8th, 8th) rnd 4 (3, 2) times more—21 (25, 29) sts.
Next rnd K to last 3 sts, ssk, k1—20 (24, 28) sts.
Work even until sleeve measures 4¾ (6, 7)"/12 (15, 18)cm from joining.
Work 2½"/(6.5)cm in k2, p2 rib. Bind off loosely in rib.

FINISHING
Block cardigan lightly to measurements.

BUTTON BAND
(left front for girls, right front for boys)
With RS facing, pick up and k 54 (62, 70) sts along desired front edge.
Next row (WS) P2, *k2, p2; rep from * to end.
K the knit sts and p the purl sts for 4 rows more.
Bind off all sts in rib.
Place markers for 7 (8, 9) buttons evenly along button band with top button in first purl rib and bottom button in last purl rib and the rem buttons evenly spaced in rem purl ribs.

BUTTONHOLE BAND
(right front for girls, left front for boys)
Pick up as for button band and work 1 row.
Next (buttonhole) row (RS) Cont in rib as established, and work buttonholes across from button markers as foll: yo, p2tog
Work 3 rows more in rib. Bind off all sts in rib. Sew on buttons opposite buttonholes. Use ends to tighten any gaps at underarm. ■

8½ (10½, 12½)"

7¼ (8½, 9½)"

5½ (6, 6½)"

4½ (5, 5½)"

5 (6, 7)"

BODY

↓ = Direction of work

18 (21, 24)"

Mini Mocs

INSPIRED BY A FAVORITE PAIR OF BOOTS, these mocs are made with a soft cotton-blend yarn to comfort baby's sensitive skin. Fringe gives a satisfying swish every time baby kicks.

SIZE
Instructions are written for size newborn to 6 months.

MEASUREMENTS
FOOT CIRCUMFERENCE:
Approx 4"/10cm
LENGTH FROM HEEL TO TOE:
3½"/9cm
LEG CIRCUMFERENCE:
Approx 6"/15cm
LENGTH FROM BOTTOM OF
HEEL TO TOP OF LEG:
6"/15cm

MATERIALS
■ 1 2.4oz /70g skein (each 282yd/258m) of Bernat *Cotton-ish by Vickie Howell* (cotton/acrylic) in #16208585012 Coffee Filter ③

■ One set (5) size 5 (3.75mm) double-pointed needles (dpns) *or size to obtain gauge*

■ Round, removeable stitch markers

■ Fabric scraps (optional)

■ Sewing needle and thread (optional)

GAUGE
■ 14 sts and 28 rows to 4"/10cm over garter stitch using size 5 (3.75mm) needles.
Take time to check your gauge.

STITCH GLOSSARY
ML (make loop) K1, leaving st on LH needle, bring yarn to front between sts, wrap yarn clockwise around your thumb to form loop, bring yarn to back and k same stitch, lift first st over the 2nd st on RH needle, and let it drop off.

SHOES (MAKE 2)
SOLE
Cast on 43 sts.
Knit 18 rows. Bind off. Place marker (pm) to indicate RS.

INSTEP
With RS facing, pm on each side of center 11 sts of bound-off edge. Working into purl bumps on WS of row below bound-off row, pick up and k 11 sts.
Knit 11 rows.
Using mattress stitch in the back loop of st only (for exposed seam), sew sides of instep to sides of sole. Sew back seam.

CUFF
Pick up and k 30 sts evenly around foot opening, dividing sts evenly on 3 dpns. Join and place marker for beg of rnd.
Work 4 rnds in garter st (k 1 rnd, p 1 rnd).
Next rnd *ML in every st around.
Next rnd Purl.
Rep last 2 rnds twice more.** Work 6 rnds in garter stitch.*
Rep from * to * once, then rep from * to ** once.
Work 2 rnds in garter st.
Next rnd *K1, p1; rep from * around.
Rep last rnd 3 times more for rib. Bind off in rib.

FINISHING
Cut loops open to create fringe. Trim to make even.

EMBELLISHMENT (OPTIONAL)
Using template, cut 2 pieces of scrap fabric. Sew one piece of fabric to each instep. ■

TEMPLATE

Biased Baby Blanket

KNITTING ON THE BIAS kicks basic garter stitch up a notch. Rows of textural garter bumps worked in a bulky, nubby yarn make for a modern-looking blanket with crib appeal.

MEASUREMENTS
Approx 36 x 37"/91.5 x 94cm

MATERIALS
■ 1 3½oz/100g skein (each 109yd/100m) of Classic Elite Yarns *Verde Collection Sprout* (organic cotton) each in #4323 Burnt Orange (A), #4302 Lime Juice (B), and #4375 Summer Rain (C) ⑤

■ One size 10 (6mm) circular needle, 36"/90cm long, or *size to obtain gauge*

GAUGE
■ 12 sts and 24 rows to 4"/10cm over garter st using size 10 (6mm) needles.
Take time to check your gauge.

STRIPE SEQUENCE
6 rows A, 6 rows B, 6 rows C.
8 rows A, 8 rows B, 8 rows C.
10 rows A, 10 rows B, 10 rows C.
12 rows A, 12 rows B, 12 rows C.
14 rows A, 14 rows B, 14 rows C.
14 rows C, 14 rows B, 14 rows A.
12 rows C, 12 rows B, 12 rows A.
10 rows C, 10 rows B, 10 rows A.
8 rows C, 8 rows B, 8 rows A.
6 rows C, 6 rows B, 6 rows A.

NOTES
1) Cut yarn after each stripe is complete. Do *not* carry colors up the side.
2) Circular needle is used to accommodate large number of sts. Do *not* join.

BLANKET
With A, cast on 4 sts.

BEG STRIPE SEQUENCE
Next (inc) row (RS) K1, kfb, k to last 2 sts, kfb, k1—2 sts inc'd.
Cont in garter st (k every row) and rep inc row every other row 74 times more—154 sts. Knit 1 row C. This is the center of the afghan and 150 rows have been worked.
Cont in stripe sequence as foll:
Next (dec) row (RS) K1, k2tog, k to last 3 sts, k2tog, k1—2 sts dec'd.
Cont in garter st and rep dec row every other row 74 times more until rem stripe sequence is complete—4 sts. Bind off with A.

FINISHING
Weave in ends. ■

Bandit Bib

BANDIT-STYLE KERCHIEFS ARE ALL THE RAGE, adding a splash of color without the commitment of a full-sized scarf. Now baby can get in on the trend with this bib-sized take on the adult favorite.

MEASUREMENTS
WIDTH (INCLUDING BUTTON TABS):
Approx 20"/51cm
LENGTH:
Approx 8"/20.5cm

MATERIALS
■ 1 2.4oz/70g skein
(each 82yd/v 258m) of Bernat
Cotton-ish by Vickie Howell
(cotton/acrylic) each in
#16208585040 Cotton Club (A)
OR #16208585416 Cotton Candy
(A) and #16208585008
Cotton Ball (B) 🧶

■ One pair size 5 (3.75mm) needles
or size to obtain gauge

■ One ¾"/2cm button

■ Sewing needle and thread

GAUGE
24 sts and 48 rows to 4"/10cm
over garter stitch using size 5
(3.75mm) needles.
Take time to check your gauge.

BIB
With A, cast on 3 sts.
Row 1 (inc RS) Kfb, k1, kfb—5 sts.
Row 2 Knit.
Next (inc) row (RS) Kfb, k to last st, kfb—2 sts inc'd.
Cont in garter st (k every row), rep inc row every other row 11 times more—29 sts.
Knit 1 row.
Cut B; join A.
Cont to work in garter st and rep inc row every other row 28 times more—85 sts.
Knit 1 row.

BORDER
Work 8 rows even in garter st. Bind off, but do not fasten off last st.

BUTTONHOLE TAB
With rem st on needle, pick up and k 5 sts along side edge of border—6 sts.
Work even in garter st until tab measures 1½"/4 cm, end with a WS row.
Next (buttonhole) row (RS) K2, bind off 2 sts, k2.
Next Row K2, cast on 2 sts, k2.
Work 4 rows even. Bind off.

BUTTON TAB
With RS facing, pick up and k 6 sts along side edge of opposite border. Work even until button tab measures same as buttonhole tab. Bind off.

FINISHING
Sew button to button tab to correspond to buttonhole. ■

Front

Back

Birthday Baby Crown

A CLEVER SERIES OF YARN-OVERS AND BIND-OFFS create the regal peaks and valleys in this knitted crown. Embellish with tulle, add a letter or number, and your kiddo will be ready to hold court!

SIZE
Instructions are written for Toddler size.

MEASUREMENTS
CIRCUMFERENCE:
Approx 14"/35.5cm
LENGTH:
Approx 5¼"/13.5cm

MATERIALS
■ 1 3½oz /100g skein
(each 210yd/192m) of Patons
Classic Wool Worsted (wool)
in #24407777418 Coral OR
#24407777219 Sea Foam (4)

■ One pair size 7 (4.5mm) needles
or size to obtain gauge

■ Size G/6 (4mm) crochet hook

■ Small amount of sequin trim

■ Small amount of gold tulle or gold gossamer fabric

■ 1 package of fabric-covered floral wire

■ Sewing needle and thread

■ Hot glue and glue gun (optional)

■ Stitch marker

GAUGE
■ 17 sts and 34 rows to
4"/10cm over garter stitch using
size 7 (4.5mm) needles.
Take time to check your gauge.

CROWN
Cast on 17 sts.
Knit 2 rows.

SHAPE POINTS
*Next (inc) row (RS) K5, yo,
k to end.
Cont in garter st, rep inc row every
other row 6 times more—24 sts.
Knit 1 row.
Next row (RS) Bind off 7 sts,
k to end.
Knit 1 row.
Rep from * 6 times more—7 points.
Bind off.

EDGE
With crochet hook, join yarn at top edge with a slip stitch. Holding floral wire parallel to edge, ch 1, sc (see page 92) around wire in each garter ridge along entire top edge, working 3 sc in tip of each point.
Fasten off. Trim wire, folding edge to secure.

FINISHING
Sew cast-on edge to bound-off edge to form crown.

APPLIQUÉ
Hot glue or hand sew sequin trim in shape of desired number or letter to center of crown.

TRIM
Cut fabric into 11 squares each measuring approx 3"/8cm. Pinch square at center and hand sew to underside of bottom edge of crown. Repeat evenly around. ■

Stroll Patrol Blanket

WHETHER IT'S TO THROW IN A DIAPER BAG, drape over a baby carrier, or lay across your little one's lap, Stroll Patrol offers a lacy, bite-sized bit of bundled-up for those everyday, chilly occasions.

MEASUREMENTS
Approx. 25 x 25"/63.5 x 63.5cm

MATERIALS
■ 3 3½oz/100g hanks (each 225yd/206m) of Madeleine Tosh *Merino DK* (superwash merino wool) in Holi Festival ⓷

■ Two size 7 (4.5mm) circular needles, 32"/80cm long, *or size to obtain gauge*

■ Scrap yarn

■ Tapestry needle

GAUGE
■ 18 sts and 36 rows to 4"/10cm over pattern st using size 7 (4.5mm) needles.
Take time to check your gauge.

PATTERN STITCH
(multiple of 10 sts plus 7)
Row 1 (RS) Knit.
Row 2 Knit.
Row 3 K4, *yo, k3, k3tog, k3, yo, k1; rep from *, end k3.
Row 4 Knit.
Rep rows 1–4 for pat st.

NOTES
1) Blanket is worked in 2 pieces and joined using garter Kitchener stitch when knitting is complete.
2) Circular needles are used to accommodate large number of stitches. Do *not* join.

BLANKET
FIRST PIECE
Cast on 117 sts.
Knit 2 rows.
Beg pat st.
Rep rows 1–4 of pat st until piece measures approx 12½"/32cm from beg.
Leave sts on needle, set aside.

SECOND PIECE
On second circular needle, work same as first piece.

FINISHING
Using garter Kitchener stitch (see pages 88–89), graft 2 pieces tog. Block to measurements. ■

Snow Leopard Sweetie Bonnet

THIS FELINE-INSPIRED BONNET is equal parts strength and beauty, just like the modern little lady who wears it. Knit it up quickly in basic garter stitch, then adorn with wee ears and cross-stitched spots.

SIZE
Instructions are written for size 0–6 months.

MEASUREMENTS
FRONT EDGE TO CENTER BACK: 6"/15cm
LENGTH: 6½"/16.5cm

MATERIALS
■ 1 3½oz/100g skein (each 210yd/192m) of Patons *Classic Wool Worsted* (wool) in #24407700202 Aran (A)

■ Small amounts in #24407700226 Black (B) and #24407777215 Heath Heather (C)

■ One pair size 7 (4.5mm) needles *or size to obtain gauge*

■ One set (2) size 7 (4.5mm) double-pointed needles (dpns)

GAUGE
■ 20 sts and 40 rows to 4"/10cm over garter st using size 7 (4.5mm) needles.
Take time to check your gauge.

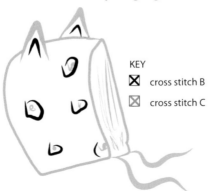

HAT
With A, cast on 62 sts.
Row 1 (RS) *K2, p2; rep from *, end k2.
Row 2 *P2, k2; rep from *, end p2.
Rep rows 1 and 2 once more.
Next row (RS) Knit.
Next row P2, k to last 2 sts, p2.
Rep last 2 rows until piece measures 4"/10cm from beg.
Cont in garter st as established, binding off 23 sts at beg of next 2 rows.

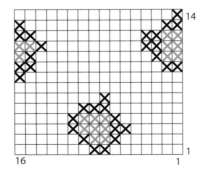

KEY
☒ cross stitch B
☒ cross stitch C

BACK FLAP
Cont in garter st on rem 16 sts until flap measures approx 4"/10cm from bound-off row, end with a WS row.
Next row (RS) *K1, p1; rep from * to end.
Rep last row for rib until back flap measures 4½"/11.5cm from bound-off row. Bind off in rib.

FINISHING
Sew sides of back flap to bound-off edges.

EARS (MAKE 2)
With A, cast on 14 sts.
Knit 2 rows.
Next (dec) row (RS) K1, k2tog tbl, k to last 3 sts, k2tog, k1—2 sts dec'd.
Cont in garter st, rep dec row every other row 4 times more—4 sts.
Knit 1 row.
Next (dec) row (RS) K1, k2tog, k1—3 sts.
Next row K3tog and fasten off.
Sew ears to top of bonnet.

I-CORD TIES (MAKE 2)
With dpns and A, pick up and k 2 sts along the 2-st St st edge.
*With A, k2, slide sts to opposite end of needle and pull yarn snuggly to work next row from RS.
Next row With C, k2, slide sts to opposite end of needle to work next row from RS; rep from *until cord measures 9"/23cm.
Bind off. Trim tail. Rep on other side of bonnet.

SPOTS
Using photos as guide, cross stitch leopard spots on bonnet, foll chart. ■

Breezy Baby Beach Pullover

EVEN IN THE HEIGHT OF SUMMER, YOU'LL SOMETIMES FEEL A CHILL NEAR THE SEA. This lightweight, cotton-blend sweater is perfect to pull over t-shirts and baby board shorts on a cool summer night.

SIZES
Instructions are written for 3 months (6 months, 12 months, 2T). Shown in size 3 months.

MEASUREMENTS
CHEST:
18 (19, 20, 21¾)"/45.5 (48, 51, 55)cm
LENGTH:
9 (10¾, 12½, 13½)"/23 (27.5, 31.5, 34.5)cm
UPPER ARM:
6¼ (7, 7½, 8½)"/16 (18, 19, 21.5)cm

MATERIALS
■ 1 (1, 2, 2) 2.4oz/70g skeins (each 282yds/258m) of Bernat *Cotton-ish by Vickie Howell* (acrylic/cotton) in each of #16208585040 Cotton Club (A) and #16208585008 Cotton Ball (B) 🔢

■ 1 skein in #16208585734 Turquoise Terry Cloth (C)

■ One size 5 (3.75mm) circular needle, 16"/40cm long, *or size needed to obtain gauge*

■ One set (5) size 5 (3.75mm) double-pointed needles (dpns)

■ 5 stitch markers

■ Scrap yarn

GAUGE
18 sts and 36 rnds to 4"/10cm over garter st using size 5 (3.75mm) needles.
Take time to check your gauge.

STRIPE PATTERN 1
4 rnds B, 4 rnds A.
Rep these 8 rnds for stripe pat 1.

STRIPE PATTERN 2
[2 rnds B, 2 rnds A] twice, 6 rnds C, 2 rnds A, 6 rnds C, 2 rnds A, [2 rnds B, 2 rnds A] twice.
Work these 32 rnds for stripe pat 2.

■ PATTERN NOTES
1) Pullover is worked in the round from the neck down.
2) Change colors on knit rnds *only*.

SWEATER
NECK
With dpns and A, cast on 66 sts. Join, taking care not to twist sts, and place marker (pm) for beg of rnd. Work in garter st (k 1 rnd, p 1 rnd) for 1"/2.5cm, end with a knit rnd.

Boatneck collars are perfect for wee babies with bigger heads!

SHAPE YOKE AND BEG STRIPE PAT 1

Note Change to circular needle when sts no longer fit comfortably on dpns.

Set-up rnd P11 (for left half of back), pm, p11 (for left sleeve), pm, p22 (for front), pm, p11 sts (for right sleeve), pm, p11 (for right half of back).

Inc rnd With B, [k to marker, yo, sl marker, k1, yo] 4 times, k to end—8 sts inc'd.

Cont in stripe pat 1 and garter st, rep inc rnd every other rnd 7 (8, 9, 11) times more, end with a purl rnd—130 (138, 146, 162) sts.

BODY

Cont in garter st and stripe pat 1.

Next rnd [K to marker, place 27 (29, 31, 35) sts on scrap yarn for sleeve] twice, k to end—76 (80, 84, 92) sts in rnd.

Next rnd P19 (20, 21, 23), cast on 3 sts for underarm, p38 (40, 42, 46), cast on 3 sts for underarm, p to end—82 (86, 90, 98) sts.

Cont in garter st and stripe pat 1 until the 8 rnds of stripe pat 1 have been completed 5 (7, 9, 10) times. Piece measures approx 5½ (7¼, 9, 10)"/14 (18.5, 23, 25.5)cm from beg.

BEG STRIPE PAT 2

Cont in garter st and work the 32 rnds of stripe pat 2. Bind off.

SLEEVES (MAKE 2)

With dpns and A, k27 (29, 31, 35) sleeve sts from scrap yarn, pick up and k 3 sts along underarm, pm for beg of rnd—30 (32, 34, 38) sts. Work even in garter st in stripe pat as foll: *2 rnds A, 2 rnds B; rep from * until sleeve measures 5 (5½, 6½, 7½)"/12.5 (14, 16.5, 19cm), end with a purl rnd in B. Cut A and B. With C, work in garter st for 1"/2.5cm. Bind off.

FINISHING

Sew underarm seams. ■

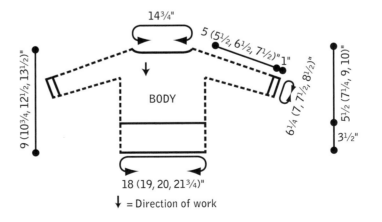

14¾"

5 (5½, 6½, 7½)"1"

9 (10¾, 12½, 13½)"

6¼ (7, 7½, 8½)"

5½ (7¼, 9, 10)"

3½"

BODY

18 (19, 20, 21¾)"

↓ = Direction of work

52

Poncho Pal

BECAUSE WRANGLING LITTLE ONES INTO WARM CLOTHING is a challenge, a good poncho is a parent's best friend. This one comes with a hood for added coverage, the perfect solution for keeping an active kid cozy.

SIZES
Instructions are written for size 12/18 months (2T/4T). Shown in size 12/18 months.

MEASUREMENTS
WIDTH:
13 (16)"/33 (40.5)cm
LENGTH (EXCLUDING HOOD):
12 (14)"/30.3 (35.5)cm

MATERIALS
■ 2 (3) 3½oz/100g skeins (each 210yd/192m) of Malabrigo *Worsted* (merino wool) in #MM125 Mariposa (4)

■ One pair size 9 (5.5mm) needles *or size to obtain gauge*

■ One spare size 9 (5.5mm) needle (for 3-needle bind-off)

■ Two 1"/2.5cm buttons

■ Scrap yarn

■ Piece of cardboard 3½"/9cm x 2"/5cm (for tassel)

GAUGE
■ 17 sts and 32 rows to 4"/10cm over garter rib using size 9 (5.5mm) needles. *Take time to check your gauge.*

GARTER RIB
(multiple of 6 sts, plus 1)
Rows 1, 3 and 5 (RS) Knit.
Rows 2, 4 and 6 P1, *K5, p1; rep from * to end.
Rep rows 1–6 for garter rib.

BACK
Cast on 55 (67) sts.
Rows 1, 3 and 5 (RS) Knit.
Rows 2 and 4 K6 (edging), p1, [k5, p1] 7 (9) times, k6 (edging).
Row 6 P6, p1, [k5, p1] 7 (9) times, p6.
Rep rows 1–6 until piece measures 11 (13)"/28 (33)cm from beg, end with a WS row.

SHAPE NECK AND SHOULDERS
Next row (RS) K16 (19), join a 2nd ball of yarn and bind off 23 (29) sts, work to end.
Working both sides at once with separate balls of yarn, cont in pat until piece measures 12 (14)"/30.5 (35.5)cm from beg. Bind off.

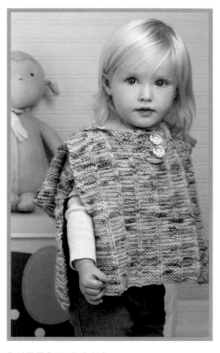

FRONT

Cast on 55 (67) sts.
Work as for back until piece measures 8½ (10½)"/21.5 (26)cm from beg, end with a WS row.

SPLIT NECK AND LEFT SHOULDER

Next row (RS) K31 (37), turn, place rem 24 (30) sts on st holder for right shoulder.
Cont in pat on 31 (37) sts only, until piece measures 10½ (12½)"/26.5 (31.5)cm from beg, end with a RS row.
Next row (WS) Bind off 12 sts, work to end—19 (25) sts.
Next row Knit to last 3 (6) sts, place these 3 (6) sts on scrap yarn to hold. Work even in pat on rem 16 (19) sts until piece measures same as back to shoulder. Bind off.

RIGHT SHOULDER

Place 24 (30) shoulder sts on needle, ready to work a RS row. Work in pat until piece measures 10½ (12½)"/26.5 (31.5)cm from beg, end with a WS row.
Next row (RS) Bind off 5 sts, work to end—19 (25) sts.
Next row (WS) Work to last 3 (6) sts, turn, place these 3 (6) sts on scrap yarn to hold—16 (19) sts.
Cont in pat until piece measures same as back to shoulder. Bind off.

BUTTON BAND

Cast on 7 sts.
Rows 1–4 Knit.
Row 5 K2, bind off 3 sts, k2.
Row 6 P2, cast on 3 sts, p2.
Rep rows 1–6 once, then rep rows 1–4 once more.
Bind off. Sew side edge of button band to right front edge of neck opening.

HOOD

Sew shoulder seams.
Note A few short rows are worked at the nape of neck of hood for subtle shaping.
With RS facing, beg at right side of neck, k 3 (6) sts from scrap yarn, pick up and k 46 (52) sts evenly along neck edge, k3 (6) sts from scrap yarn—52 (64) sts.
Row 1 (WS) Knit.
Row 2 K32 (38), turn, leaving rem sts unworked.
Row 3 K11, turn.
Row 4 K7, turn.
Row 5 K3, turn.
Row 6 Knit to end.
Row 7 Knit.
Row 8 P4, k to last 4 sts, p4.
Rows 9–13 Knit.

Row 14 Rep row 8.
Rep rows 9–14 until hood measures 10¼"/26cm from neck edge.

CLOSE TOP

Divide sts evenly on 2 needles and join using 3-needle bind-off (see page 90) with each WS held together so that a decorative seam shows on RS.

FINISHING

Sew buttons to left side of neck split to correspond to buttonholes.

TASSEL

Wrap yarn 18–20 times lengthwise around cardboard. Run a strand of yarn through the top loops, and tie to secure. Slide yarn off card and wrap a strand of yarn several times around tassel approx ½"/1cm down from top. Tie to secure. Cut loops at opposite end and trim to make even. Feed strand at top of tassel through top corner of hood and secure on WS. ∎

Sherbet Scoop Garland

HALF-CIRCLE, BI-COLORED MOTIFS PAIRED WITH VELVETEEN RIBBON make a sweet swag. From newborn's nursery to pre-k classroom, this bunting will add a pop of color to any space.

MEASUREMENTS
5 scallop garland is approx 68"/172.5cm long

MATERIALS
■ 1 3½oz/100g skein (each 210yd/192m) of Patons *Classic Wool Worsted* (wool) in #24407777418 Coral (A) 🧶

■ 1 3oz/85g skein (each 167yd/153m) of Bernat *Sheep-ish by Vickie Howell* (acrylic/wool) in 00021 Raspberry(ish) (B) 🧶

■ One pair size 8 (5mm) needles *or size to obtain gauge*

■ 2yd/1m of ¼"/.5cm velvet ribbon

■ Sewing needle and thread

GAUGES
■ 16 sts and 32 rows to 4"/10cm over garter st using size 8 (5mm) needles.
■ 1 scallop is approx 7"/18cm across flat edge and 4½"/11.5cm long at longest point.
Take time to check your gauges.

SCALLOP (MAKE 5)
With A, cast on 16 sts.
Row 1 (RS) K15, sl 1, bring yarn to front and return sl st to LH needle, turn (last st is wrapped), k to end.
Row 2 K13, sl 1, bring yarn to front and return sl st to LH needle, turn, k to end.
Row 3 K11, sl 1, bring yarn to front and return sl st to LH needle, turn, k to end.
Row 4 K9, sl 1, bring yarn to front and return sl st to LH needle, turn, k to end.
Row 5 K7, sl 1, bring yarn to front and return sl st to LH needle, turn, k to end.
Row 6 K5, sl 1, bring yarn to front and return sl st to LH needle, turn, k to end.
Row 7 K3, sl 1, bring yarn to front and return sl st to LH needle, turn, k to end.

Row 8 K1, sl 1, bring yarn to front and return sl st to LH needle, turn, k to end.
Rep rows 1–8 twice more.
Cut A; join B. Rep Rows 1–8 three times more.

TOP BORDER
Cont with B, k16 (first half of top), pick up and k 15 sts evenly across 2nd half of top.
Knit 3 rows.
Bind off.

FINISHING
Fold each end of ribbon approx 2"/5cm and tack to form loops. Beg approx 8½"/21.5cm from end of 1 loop, sew first scallop to ribbon along top edge. Leaving approx 4"/10cm between each scallop, sew rem scallops to ribbon. ■

■ **ANOTHER GREAT YARN OPTION!**
Classic Elite Minnow Merino By Jill Eaton

■ **TIP**
Try switching things up with a scallop or two or three in different colors!

Good Lad Baby Shoes

IF YOU'VE HAD TROUBLE FINDING BITTY BOOTIES FOR BOY BABIES, you'll love the Good Lad shoes. Customize them a nearly infinite number of ways with different fabric, buckles, and button adornments.

SIZE
Instructions are written for size 6 months.

MEASUREMENTS
LENGTH FROM HEEL TO TOE: 3½"/9cm

MATERIALS
■ 1 1¾oz/50g skein (each 140yd/128m) of Brooklyn Tweed *Shelter* (wool) in Graphite (4)

■ One set (5) size 7 (4.5mm) double-pointed needles (dpns) *or size to obtain gauge*

■ Small amount of faux leather fabric

■ 2 vintage buttons

■ Sewing needle and thread OR sewing machine

■ Stitch markers

GAUGE
■ 20 sts and 40 rows to 4"/10cm over garter stitch using size 7 (4.5mm) needles.
Take time to check your gauge.

NOTE
Sole of shoe is worked in rows; top of shoe is worked in rounds.

SHOES
SOLE
With 2 dpns, cast on 5 sts.
Do *not* join.
Knit 2 rows.
Next (inc) rnd (RS) Kfb, k to last st, kfb—7 sts.
Knit 1 row.
Cont in garter st (k every row), rep inc row every 4th row once, then every 6th row once—11 sts.
Work even until piece measures 3¼"/8.5cm, end with a WS row.
Next (dec) row (RS) K2tog tbl, k to last 2 sts, k2tog—9 sts.
Rep dec row every other row once more—7 sts.
Knit 1 row. Bind off.

■
Go, good lass by choosing more femme colors.

SHOE TOP
With 4 dpns, pick up and k 48 sts evenly around entire edge of sole. Join and place marker (pm) for beg of rnd.
Next rnd K21, pm, k6, pm, k21.
Work 3 rnds more in garter st (k 1 rnd, p 1 rnd).
Next (dec) rnds K to 2 sts before marker, k2tog, sl marker, k to next marker, sl marker, k2tog, k to end—2 sts dec'd.
Cont in garter st, rep dec rnd every other rnd 5 times more—36 sts.
Purl 1 rnd.
Next (dec) rnd K to 2 sts before marker, k2tog, sl marker, k2, k2tog, k2, sl marker, k2tog, k to end—33 sts.
Purl 1 rnd. Bind off.

FINISHING
STRAPS
Cut 4 pieces of faux leather approx 4"/10cm long by 1¼"/3cm wide. With WS tog, machine or hand-sew 2 pieces together. Rep for rem pieces.
Using photo as guide, lay strap across top of shoe and sew one end to bottom of shoe. Place button on opposite end of strap and sew button to shoe through strap. Rep for 2nd shoe. ■

Patched Pants

AS TYKE BECOMES TODDLER, he'll need some crawl-ready pants. This denim-look pair is armed (legged?) with patches that reinforce the knit fabric while keeping his commitment to cool.

SIZES
Instructions are written for size 6 months (12 months, 24 months). Shown in size 12 months.

MEASUREMENTS
HIP CIRCUMFERENCE:
21 (21, 23)"/53.5 (53.5, 58.5)cm
LENGTH:
13 (14, 15)"/33 (35.5, 38)cm

MATERIALS
■ 1 (1, 2) 3oz/85g skeins (each 144yds/132m) of Patons *Denim-y* (cotton/wool/acrylic) in #24409696115 Medium Blue Denim **(4)**

■ One each sizes 7 and 8 (4.5 and 5mm) circular needle, 16"/40cm long, *or size to obtain gauge*

■ Size H/8 (5mm) crochet hook

■ Stitch marker

■ Small amount of home-décor weight fabric

■ Small amount of fusible webbing

■ Sewing thread and needle OR sewing machine

GAUGE
13 sts and 26 rnds to 4"/10cm over garter st using larger needle.
Take time to check your gauge.

K1, P1 RIB
(over an even number of sts)
Rnd 1 *K1, p1; rep from * around.
Rep rnd 1 for k1, p1 rib.

PANTS
With smaller needle, cast on 64 (68, 74) sts. Join, being careful not to twist sts, and place marker (pm) for beg of rnd.
Work 4 rnds in k1, p1 rib.

WAISTBAND
Next (eyelet) rnd *Yo, k2tog; rep from * around.
Change to larger needle.
For 6 months size only:
Next row Purl, inc 4 sts evenly around—68 sts.
For 12 months and 24 months sizes only:
Next row Purl.

NOTE
Pants are knit in the round from the waist down, then right and left legs are knit separately, working back and forth, and seamed.

For all sizes:
Work in garter st (k 1 rnd, p 1 rnd) until piece measures 6 (6½, 7)"/15 (16.5, 18)cm from beg, end with a purl rnd.

DIVIDE FOR LEGS
Dividing row K34 (34, 37), turn, place rem sts on scrap yarn to hold for left leg.

RIGHT LEG
Cont on 34 (34, 37) sts for right leg only, work in garter st in rows (k every row) as foll:
Next row (WS) Bind off 2 sts, k to end—32 (32, 35) sts.
Next row Bind off 1 st, k to end—31 (31, 34) sts.
Work even in garter st until leg measures 7 (7½, 8)"/18 (19, 20.5)cm or desired length from dividing row. Bind off loosely.

LEFT LEG
Place 34 (34, 37) sts from scrap yarn on needle.
Next row (RS) Bind off 1 st, k to end—33 (33, 36) sts.
Next row (WS) Bind off 2 sts, k to end—31 (31, 34) sts.
Complete as for right leg.

FINISHING
KNEE PATCHES
Cut 2 fabric circles each with a
2½"/6.5cm diameter (the bottom
of a juice glass makes a great patch
template!). Rep for fusible webbing.
Following manufacturer's
instructions, apply fusible webbing to
WS of fabric patches.
Using photo as guide, sew patches to
knees with machine or by hand.
Sew inseam.

CORD
Crochet a chain approx 26
(27, 28)"/66 (68.5, 71)cm long.
Weave cord through eyelets and tie
in bow to wear. ■

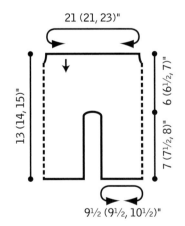

21 (21, 23)"

13 (14, 15)"

6 (6½, 7)"

7 (7½, 8)"

9½ (9½, 10½)"

↓ = Direction of work

Honey Baby Pullover

UP THE MOD FACTOR on a traditional Aran honeycomb pattern by knitting it in lime-green garter stitch. Pair with contrasting sleeve stripes, and you've got a snazzy sweater that will melt a mama's heart.

SIZES
Instructions are written for size 12 months (2T, 4T). Shown in size 12 months.

MEASUREMENTS
CHEST:
21 (24, 26)"/53.5 (61, 68.5)cm
LENGTH:
12 (13, 14)"/30.5 (33, 35.5)cm
UPPER ARM:
7½ (8½, 8 ¾)"/19 (21.5, 22)cm

MATERIALS
■ 1 (1, 2) 2.4oz/70g skeins (each 210yd/192m) of Patons *Classic Wool Worsted* (wool) in #24407777223 Lemongrass (A) ④

■ 1 skein each in #24407700201 Winter White (B) and #24407700226 Black (C)

■ One pair each sizes 6 and 7 (4 and 4.5mm) needles *or size needed to obtain gauge*

■ Cable needle (cn)

■ Stitch holders

GAUGES
■ 20 sts and 40 rows to 4"/10cm over garter stitch using smaller needles.
■ 28 sts and 40 rows to 4"/10cm over honeycomb garter st using larger needles.
Take time to check your gauges.

SLEEVE STRIPE PATTERN
(over any number of sts)
Knit 2 rows B, knit 2 rows C.
Rep these 4 rows for sleeve stripe pat.

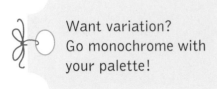
Want variation?
Go monochrome with
your palette!

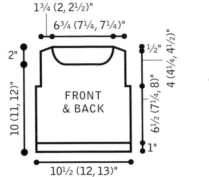

1¾ (2, 2½)"
6¾ (7¼, 7¼)"
2"
½"
4 (4¼, 4½)"
FRONT & BACK
10 (11, 12)"
6½ (7¼, 8)"
1"
10½ (12, 13)"

7½ (8½, 8¾)"
SLEEVE
6 (8, 10)"
1"
4½ (5½, 6)"

BACK
With larger needles and A, cast on 55 (63, 71) sts.
Row 1 (RS) Knit.
Row 2 *K3, p1; rep from * to last 3 sts, k3.
Rep rows 1 and 2 until piece measures 1"/2.5cm from beg, end with a RS row.
Next (inc) row (WS) K1, M1, k6, p1, k18 (23, 27), M1, k to last 7 sts, p1, k5, M1, k1—58 (66, 74) sts.

BEG HONEYCOMB GARTER ST
Row 1 Knit.
Row 2 K8, p1, k4, *sl 2 sts to cn and hold to *back*, k2, k2 from cn, sl next 2 sts to cn and hold to *front*, k2, k2 from cn; rep from * to last 13 sts, k4, p1, k8.
Rows 3, 5 and 7 Knit.
Row 4 K8, p1, k4, k to last 13 sts, k4, p1, k8.
Row 6 K8, p1, k4, *sl 2 sts to cn and hold to *front*, k2, k2 from cn, sl 2 sts to cn and hold to *back*, k2, k2 from cn; rep from * to last 13 sts, k4, p1, k8.
Row 8 Rep row 4.
Rep rows 1–8 for honeycomb garter st until piece measures 7½" (8 ¼, 9)"/19 (21, 23)cm from beg.

SHAPE ARMHOLE
Bind off 4 sts at beg of next 2 rows, then 0 (1, 3) sts at beg of next 2 rows—50 (56, 60) sts.
Work even in pat as established until piece measures 11 ½ (12½, 13 ½)"/29 (31.5, 34.5)cm from beg, end with a WS row.

SHAPE SHOULDERS
Bind off 4 (5, 6) sts at beg of next 4 rows. Place rem 34 (36, 36) sts on stitch holder for back neck.

FRONT
Work as for back until piece measures 10 (11, 12)"/25.5 (28, 30.5)cm from beg, end with a WS row.

SHAPE LEFT NECK AND SHOULDER
Next row (RS) K13 (15, 17) sts, place center 24 (26, 26) sts on st holder for front neck, join a 2nd ball of yarn and k to end.
Working both sides at once with separate balls of yarn, cont in pat as established, dec 1 st at each neck edge every other row 5 times—8 (10, 12) sts rem each side.
When piece measures same as back to shoulder, shape shoulders as for back.

SLEEVES (MAKE 2)
With smaller needles and B, cast on 23 (27, 31) sts.
Row 1 (RS) Knit.
Row 2 *K3, p1; rep from * to last 3 sts, k3.
Rep rows 1 and 2 twice more.

BEG SLEEVE STRIPE PAT
Join C and work in sleeve stripe pat, inc 1 st each side every 6th (0, 0) row 2 (0, 0) times, then every 8th (10th, 14th) row 5 (7, 6) times—37 (41, 43) sts.
Work even in stripe pat until piece measures 7 (9, 11)"/18 (23, 28)cm from beg.
Bind off.

FINISHING
Sew right shoulder seam.

NECKBAND
With RS facing, smaller needles and A, beg at left front neck, pick up and k 7 (9, 9) sts along neck edge, k24 (26, 26) from front neck holder, pick up and k 7 (9, 9) sts along right neck edge, k34 (36, 36) from back neck holder—72 (80, 80) sts.
Row 1 (WS): *K3, p1; rep from * to end.
Row 2 Knit.
Rep row 1 once more. Change to larger needle to bind off.
Sew left shoulder and neckband seam. Sew sleeves into armholes. Sew side and sleeve seams. ∎

Gaga Glam Cloche

AS WONDERFUL AS THE JOURNEY IS, MOTHERHOOD isn't always full of glamour. At least, though, our peewee prodigies can look the glam part wearing this warm cloche bursting with art deco-inspired style.

SIZE
Instructions are written for size 12-18 months.

MEASUREMENTS
HEAD CIRCUMFERENCE:
16"/40cm
Length:
5½"/14cm

MATERIALS
■ 1 3½oz/100g skein (each 143yd/131m) of Patons *Misty* (acrylic/nylon/wool/mohair) in #24109494002 Blushing Glow (A) ⑤

■ 1 3oz/85g skein (each 167yd/153m) of Bernat *Sheepish by Vickie Howell* (acrylic/wool) in #16416900004 White(ish) (B) ④

■ One set (5) size 9 (5.5mm) double-pointed needles (dpns) *or size to obtain gauge*

■ 6 stitch markers

■ Beaded appliqué

■ Felt scrap

■ Fabric glue

■ Sewing needle and thread

GAUGE
14 sts and 28 rnds to 4"/10cm over garter st using size 9 (5.5mm) needles and A.
Take time to check your gauge.

HAT
With A, cast on 57 sts. Join, being careful not to twist sts, pm for beg of rnd.
Rnd 1 With A, knit.
Rnd 2 Purl.
Rnd 3 Knit.
Rnd 4 Purl.
Rnds 5 and 6 With B, knit.
Rep rnds 1–6 three times more for welt pat, then rep rnds 1–5 once more. Piece measures 4"/10cm from beg.

SHAPE CROWN
Set-up rnd 1 With B, knit, dec 2 sts evenly around—55 sts.
Set-up rnd 2 K5, pm, [k11, pm] 4 times, k6.

Note The markers referred to in dec rnds do not include beg of rnd marker.
Rnd 1 (dec) With A, [k to 2 sts before marker, ssk, sl marker, k2tog] 5 times, k to end—10 sts dec'd.
Rnd 2 Purl.
Rnd 3 (dec) With B, [k to 2 sts before marker, ssk, sl marker, k2tog] 5 times, k to end—10 sts dec'd.
Rnd 4 Knit.
Rep rnds 1–4 once more—15 sts.
Next (dec) rnd With A, k1, [k2tog] 7 times around—8 sts.
Purl 1 rnd.
Cut yarn, leaving a 6"/15cm tail. Thread tail through rem sts and cinch closed.

FINISHING
Trace around appliqué on felt scrap and cut out shape. Glue felt to back of appliqué and let dry.
Hand sew appliqué to cloche, using photo as placement guide. ■

Ruffle Bum Diaper Covers

DIAPER COVERS COME ALIVE WITH ADDED FLAIR TO THE DERRIÈRE.
Trim with angular shark teeth or swaying waves for an adorable finish.

SIZE
Instructions are written for size 3 months.

MEASUREMENTS
Circumference:
14"/35.5cm

MATERIALS
■ 1 3½oz /100g hank (each 219yd/200m) of Manos del Uruguay *Maxima* (wool) in #M2169 Speeding Ticket or #M2426 Stratus (4)

■ One size 7 (4.5mm) circular needle, 16"/40cm long, *or size to obtain gauge*

■ One set (5) size 7 (4.5mm) double pointed-needles (dpns)

■ Stitch marker

■ Scrap yarn

■ Stitch holder

■ Approx ¾yd/.75m sequin and tulle trim (for ruffle version)

■ Sewing needle and thread (for ruffle version)

GAUGE
17 sts and 36 rnds to 4"/10cm over garter stitch using size 7 (4.5mm) needles.
Take time to check your gauge.

Boy Version

Front

Back

DIAPER COVER
With circular needle, cast on 60 sts. Join, being careful not to twist sts, and place marker (pm) for beg of rnd.
Rnds 1–4 *K2, p2; rep from * around.
Rnd 5 (eyelet) *K2, yo, k2tog; rep from * around.
Beg with a purl rnd, work in garter st (p 1 rnd, k 1 rnd) until piece measures 6"/15cm from beg.

DIVIDE FOR LEGS
Next rnd Place 24 sts on scrap yarn for front.
Work back and forth in rows on rem 36 sts for back as foll:
Knit 3 rows.
Next (dec) row (RS) [K2tog tbl] twice, k to last 4 sts, [k2tog] twice—4 sts dec'd.
Rep dec row every 4th row four times more—16 sts.
Knit 3 rows.

Next (inc) row (RS) K1, M1, k to last st, M1, k1—14 sts.
Knit 3 rows.
Place sts on st holder.

Place 24 sts from scrap yarn on circular needle.
Work back and forth in rows on these 24 sts for front as foll:
Knit 3 rows.
Next (dec) row (RS) [K2tog tbl] twice, k to last 4 sts, [k2tog] twice—4 sts dec'd.
Rep dec row every 4th row twice more—12 sts.
Knit 12 rows.
Next (inc) row (RS) K1, M1, k to last st, M1, k1—14 sts.
Knit 3 rows.

Zig-zag trim gives baby a little edge!

Rnds 1–5 *K2, p2; rep from *
around.
Bind off in rib.
Rep for opposite leg.

TIE
Cast on 128 sts. Bind off.
Thread tie through eyelet rnd and tie
in bow, as shown.

EMBELLISHMENT
For girl version only:
RUFFLES
Measure approx 3"/7.5cm down
from top edge at center of back.
*With RS facing, pick up and k 22 sts
evenly across back center.
Knit 3 rows.
Next (ruffle) row (RS) **K1, yo;
rep from ** across—44 sts.
Knit 1 row. Bind off.
Rep from * twice more, 4 rows down
from previous ruffle.
Using needle and thread, sew sequin
and tulle trim to edge of each ruffle.

For boy version only:
SHARK TOOTH FLAIR
(MAKE 2)
Cast on 4 sts.
Row 1 (RS) K2, yo, k2.
Row 2 and all WS rows Knit.
Row 3 K2, yo, k3.
Row 5 K2, yo, k4.
Row 7 K2, yo k5.
Row 9 Bind off 4 sts, k to end.
Row 10 Knit.
Rep rows 1–10 five times more.
Bind off.

Measure approx 3"/7.5cm down
from top edge at center back.
Sew on first flair.
Sew 2nd flair 6 rows down from
the first. ∎

Girl Version

FINISHING
GRAFT CROTCH
Place sts for back on needle.
Holding needles parallel with WS
together, graft crotch using garter
Kitchener st.

LEG BAND
With dpns, pick up and k 36 sts
evenly around leg opening;
pm for beg of rnd; join, being careful
not to twist.

Coyote Kid Sweater

INSPIRED BY COWICHAN-STYLE SWEATERS, this pint-size version couldn't be cuter. Because of the larger gauge, it's sized up for the toddler and pre-school set—knit a larger size now and display in the nursery as baby's first piece of fiber art.

SIZES
Instructions are written for size 2T (4T). Shown in size 4T.

MEASUREMENTS
CHEST:
23 (26)"/58.5 (66)cm
LENGTH:
13¼ (14½)"/33.5 (37)cm
UPPER ARM:
7¼ (8)"/18.5 (20.5)cm

MATERIALS
■ 3 3oz/100g hanks (each 78yd/71m) of Patons *Classic Wool Bulky* (wool) in #24108989008 Aran (A) ⑤

■ 1 skein each in #24108989420 Deep Blush (B), #24108989223 Spring Green (C), #24108989044 Medium Grey Heather (D), and #24108989040 Black (E)

■ One pair each sizes 10½ and 11 (6.5 and 8mm) needles *or size to obtain gauge*

■ Bobbins (optional)

■ Seven 1"/2.5cm buttons

■ Large-eyed tapestry needle

■ Sewing needle and thread

GAUGE
■ 11 sts and 20 rows to 4"/10cm over garter st using larger needles.
Take time to check your gauge.

K2, P2 RIB
(multiple of 4 sts)
Row 1 (RS) *K2, p2; rep from * to end.
Row 2 K the knit sts and p the purl sts.
Rep row 2 for k2, p2 rib.

K2, P2 RIB
(multiple of 4 sts, plus 2)
Row 1 (RS) K2, *p2, k2; rep from * to end.
Row 2 K the knit sts and p the purl sts.
Rep row 2 for k2, p2 rib.

CHECK PATTERN
(over an even number of sts)
Row 1 (RS) *K1 A, k1 E; rep from * to end.
Row 2 *K1 E, k1 A; rep from * to end.
Row 3 Rep row 2.

Row 4 Rep row 1.
These 4 rows make up the check pat.

SHORT ROW WRAP AND TURN (W&T)
Note Directions for working short row w&t on RS are given first, with directions for working on WS in parentheses.
1) Wyib (wyif), sl next st purlwise.
2) Move yarn between the needles to the front (back).
3) Sl the same st back to LH needle. Turn work, bring yarn to the RS (WS) side between needles. One st is wrapped.
4) When short rows are completed, hide all wraps as foll: work to just before wrapped st, insert RH needle knitwise (purlwise) under the wrap and into wrapped st, k (p) them together.

BACK
With A and smaller needles, cast on 32 (36) sts.
Work 6 rows in k2, p2 rib. Change to larger needles.
Knit 2 rows.

BEGIN CHART 1
Next row (RS) Beg with row 3 (row 1), work 4-st rep 8 (9) times across. Cont in garter st and work chart in this manner until row 12 (14) is complete.
With A, knit 2 rows.

BEGIN CHART 2
Note Chart 2 is worked using the intarsia method. Use a separate strand or bobbin for each color section. Do *not* carry color across the back of the work.

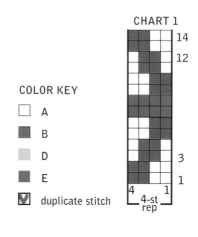

CHART 1

COLOR KEY
- ☐ A
- ■ B
- ▨ D
- ■ E
- ☑ duplicate stitch

4-st rep

CHART 2

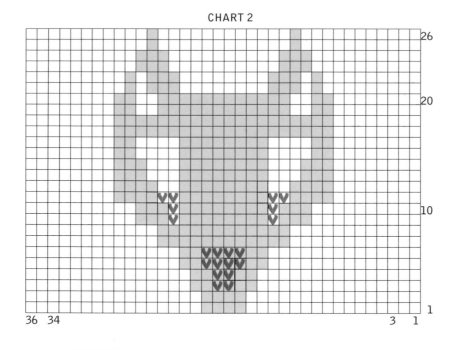

CHART 3

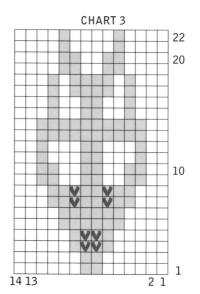

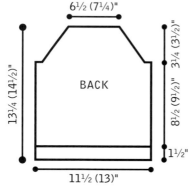

BACK

6½ (7¼)"
13¼ (14½)"
3¼ (3½)"
8½ (9½)"
1½"
11½ (13)"

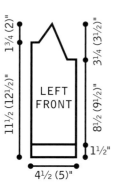

LEFT FRONT

1¾ (2)"
11½ (12½)"
3¼ (3½)"
8½ (9½)"
1½"
4½ (5)"

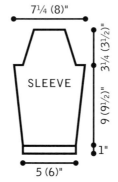

SLEEVE

7¼ (8)"
3¼ (3½)"
9 (9½)"
1"
5 (6)"

Row 1 (RS) Beg with st 3 (1), knit, foll chart through st 34 (36).
Row 2 Beg with st 34 (36), knit, foll chart through st 3 (1).
Cont to work chart in this manner until row 26 is complete.
With A, knit 2 rows.

BEGIN CHECK PAT AND SHAPE RAGLANS
Working rows 1 and 2 of check pat, bind off 2 sts at beg of next 2 rows—28 (32) sts.
Next (dec) row (RS) Working row 3 of check pat, k2tog tbl, work to last 2 sts, k2tog—2 sts dec'd.
Work row 4 of check pat.

Work in garter st and stripe pat as foll: 2 rows C, 2 rows B, cont in A to end, AT SAME TIME, dec 1 st each side as before on next row, then every other row 1 (2) times more, then every 4th row twice—18 (20) sts. Knit 1 row. Bind off.

RIGHT FRONT
With A and smaller needles, cast on 12 (14) sts.
Work 6 rows in k2, p2 rib. Change to larger needles.
Knit 2 rows.

BEGIN CHART 1
Next row (RS) Beg with row 3

(1) and st 1 (3), knit to end of rep, rep 4-st rep 2 (3) more times.
Next row (RS) Knit 4-st rep 3 times, work sts 0 (4–3) once more.
Cont in garter st, work chart in this way until row 12 (14) is complete.
With A, knit 4 rows.

BEGIN CHART 3
Row 1 (RS) Beg with st 2 (1), knit, foll chart through st 13 (14).
Row 2 Beg with st 13 (14), knit, foll chart through st 2 (1).
Cont to work chart in this manner until row 22 is complete.
With A, knit 4 rows.

Orange, instead of gray, makes this coyote cardigan foxy!

BEGIN CHECK PAT, SHAPE RAGLAN AND FRONT NECK

Work row 1 of check pat.
Next row (WS) Bind off 2 sts, work in check pat to end—10 (12) sts.
Dec row (RS) Work in check pat to last 2 sts, k2tog—9 (11) sts.
Work row 4 of check pat.
Next row (RS) With C, k to last 2 sts, k2tog—1 st dec'd.
With C, knit 1 row.
With B, rep last 2 rows once more—7 (9) sts.
Cont in garter st with A, dec 1 st at armhole edge every other row 0 (1) time more, then every 4th row twice, AT SAME TIME, bind off 2 sts at neck edge (beg of RS rows) once, then dec 1 st at neck edge every other row 2 (3) times.
When all shaping is complete, fasten off rem st.

LEFT FRONT

Work as for right front until Chart 1.

BEGIN CHART 1

Next row (RS) Beg with row 3 (1) and st 1, knit to end of rep, rep 4-st rep 2 more times, work sts 0 (1–2) once more.
Next row (RS) Work sts 0 (2–1), work 4-st rep 3 times.
Cont in garter st, work chart in this way until row 12 (14) is complete.
With A, knit 4 rows.

Work Chart 3 as for right front.

BEGIN CHECK PAT, SHAPE RAGLAN AND FRONT NECK

Next row (RS) Bind off 2 sts, work row 1 of check pat to end—10 (12) sts.

Work row 2 of check pat.
Dec row (RS) K2tog tbl, work row 3 of check pat to end—9 (11) sts.
Work row 4 of check pat.
Next row (RS) With C, k2tog tbl, k to end—1 st dec'd.
With C, knit 1 row.
With B, rep last 2 rows once more—7 (9) sts.
Cont in garter st with A, dec 1 st at armhole edge every other row 0 (1) time more, then every 4th row twice, AT SAME TIME, bind off 2 sts at neck edge (beg of WS rows) once, then dec 1 st at neck edge every other row 2 (3) times.
When all shaping is complete, fasten off rem st.

SLEEVES (MAKE 2)

With A and smaller needles, cast on 14 (16) sts.
Work in k2, p2 rib for 4 rows.
Change to larger needles.
Knit 2 rows.

BEGIN CHART 1

Next row (RS) Beg with row 3 (1), work 4-st rep 3 (4) times across, work sts 1–2 (0).
Cont in garter st to work chart in this manner until row 12 (14) is complete.

SHAPE SLEEVE

Next (inc) row (RS) With A, kfb, work chart pat to last st, kfb—2 sts inc'd.
Knit 11 rows. With D, knit 2 rows.
Rep inc row—18 (20) sts.
Knit 1 row A, 2 rows D, 2 rows A, 2 rows D, knit 6 rows A.
Rep inc row once more—20 (22) sts.
Knit 1 row A.

BEGIN CHECK PAT AND SHAPE RAGLAN

Working rows 1 and 2 of check pat, bind off 2 sts at beg of next 2 rows—16 (18) sts.
Next (dec) row (RS) K2tog tbl, work row 3 of check pat to last 2 sts, k2tog—2 sts dec'd.

Work row 4 of check pat.
Working in garter st and stripe pat as foll: 2 rows C, 2 rows B, work to end in A, AT SAME TIME, rep dec row on next row, then every other row 1 (2) times more, then every 4th row twice—6 sts.
Knit 1 row. Bind off.

SHAWL COLLAR AND BUTTONBAND

With smaller needles and A, cast on 182 (190) sts.
Row 1 (RS) *K2, p2; rep from * to last 2 sts, k2.
Row 2 *P2, k2; rep from * to last 2 sts, p2.

BEGIN SHORT ROWS

Row 3 Rib 120 (126) sts, w&t.
Row 4 Rib 60 (62) sts, w&t.
Row 5 Rib 56 (58) sts, w&t.
Row 6 Rib 52 (54) sts, w&t.
Row 7 Rib 48 (50) sts, rib to end.
Next (buttonhole) row (WS) Rib to last 60 sts, [bind off 2 sts, work in rib until there are 6 sts from bind-off] 7 times, rib to end.
Next row Rib to end, casting on 2 sts over each set of bound-off sts.
Rib 1 row. Bind off loosely in rib.

FINISHING

Block pieces.
Embroider eyes and noses using duplicate st (see page 91).
Sew in raglan sleeves. Sew side and sleeve seams.
Matching cast-on edge of shawl collar/button band to inside edge of fronts and neck, sew evenly in place.
With sewing needle and thread, sew on buttons to correspond with buttonholes. ◾

Techniques

YOU MAY BE UNFAMILIAR with some of the techniques you will encounter throughout this book. Here is a collection of step-by-step instructions to help guide you through a number of them.

Casting On

■ E-WRAP CAST-ON

The E-Wrap Cast-On is very useful and incredibly versatile. It can be used to cast on stitches at the end of rows, in the middle of rows (like for the buttonholes in the Coyote Kid Sweater, pages 71–75), or as an initial cast-on. If used for an initial cast-on, you will first need to make a slipknot and place it on the needle.

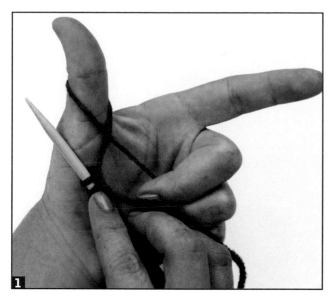

1. *Wrap the working yarn around your thumb clockwise, letting it hang. You'll see a backwards loop around your thumb that resembles a cursive, lower-case E (**e**).

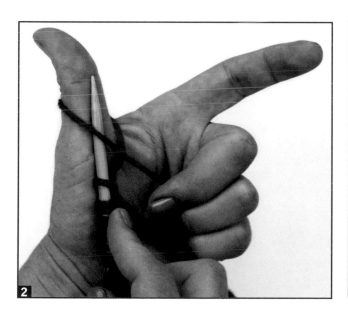

2. Insert the tip of the knitting needle up through the bottom of the loop.

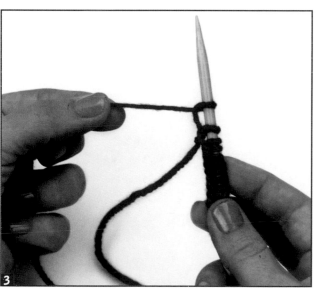

3. Remove your thumb while simultaneously pulling the working yarn so the stitch is secure (but not too tight) on the needle. Repeat from * for as many stitches as are needed.

■ PROVISIONAL CAST-ON (CROCHET CHAIN METHOD)

A provisional cast-on will keep the cast-on stitches "live" so that you can pick them up and work from them later. This method requires a crochet hook, but I think it's also the easiest to do.

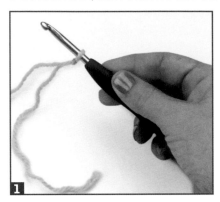

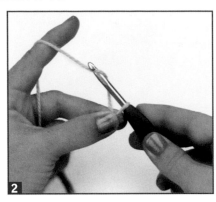

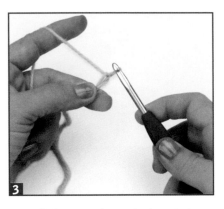

1. Using waste yarn (in the same weight as the project yarn), and an appropriately-sized crochet hook, tie a slipknot onto the hook. This will act as your first stitch.

2. *Wrap yarn counter-clockwise around the hook.

3. Pull the yarn through the stitch on the hook. Repeat from * until your chain is several stitches longer than the cast-on amount called for in the pattern. Fasten off.

4. Using project yarn and knitting needle, and beginning a few stitches from one end of the chain, pull a loop through a chain stitch and place it on the needle. Pick up as many cast-on stitches as are needed in this manner. Let the unused chain stitches hang.

You are now ready to begin working from the stitches on the needle as with any other form of cast-on. When the pattern directs, you can slip the tip of a double-pointed needle through the chain stitch that anchors each knit stitch in the first row, carefully remove the waste yarn, and end up with a row of live stitches to work from.

■ SINGLE CAST-ON

Most of the projects in this book don't require a specific cast-on method to begin them. You may use whichever method you're most comfortable with, but I personally prefer what I call the Single Cast-On method.

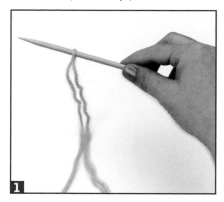

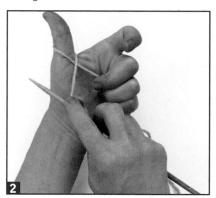

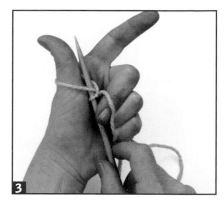

1. Begin by making a slipknot and slipping it onto one needle.

2. Allowing approximately 1"/2.5cm of yarn tail per stitch that you'll be casting on, hold tail securely with the pinky and ring finger of your left hand, and wrap the working yarn around your thumb counter-clockwise, letting it hang. You'll see a backwards loop around your thumb that resembles a cursive, lower-case E (**e**).

3. *Insert the tip of the knitting needle up through the bottom of the loop.

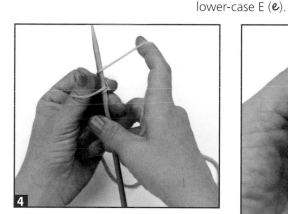

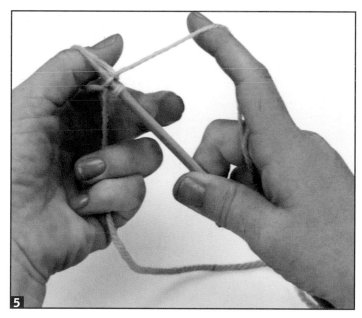

4. Holding the needle between your thumb and forefinger, wrap the working yarn around the needle clockwise.

5. Transfer the loop from your thumb onto the needle by dipping the needle into the loop and scooping it off. Repeat from * until you have cast on the desired number of stitches.

Basic Stitches

■ GARTER STITCH (FLAT)

Garter stitch worked flat is created by working the knit stitch every row, whether you're knitting on the public or non-public side of the piece. Here's how to work the knit stitch.

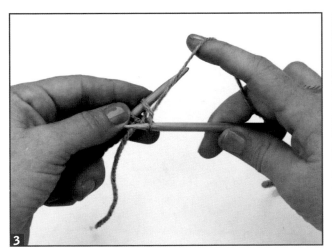

1. *Insert the right-hand needle, from front to back (knitwise), into the next stitch on the left-hand needle. The tips of your needles will form an X.

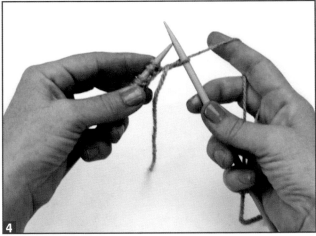

2. Bring the yarn under and then over the right-hand needle.

3. Pull the yarn on the right-hand needle through the stitch.

4. Slip the stitch off the left-hand needle. Repeat from * for as many stitches as are needed.

■ GARTER STITCH (IN THE ROUND)

To create garter stitch when working in the round, you must alternate one knit round with one purl round. See the previous page for instructions on working the knit stitch. Here's how to work the purl stitch.

1. *With yarn in front, insert the right-hand needle into the stitch from back to front (purlwise).

2. Bring the yarn over and then under the right-hand needle.

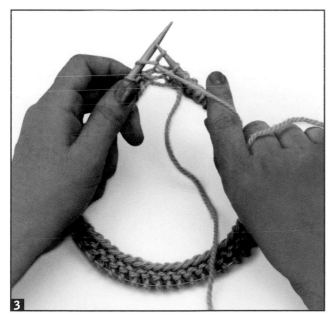

3. Pull the yarn through the stitch with the right-hand needle.

4. Slip the stitch off the left-hand needle. Repeat from * for as many stitches as are needed.

■ I-CORD

Knowing how to make an I-cord will come in handy for many of your knitting projects. The instructions below create a tube of stockinette stitch, perfect for ties. To make a garter stitch version, simply purl every other row.

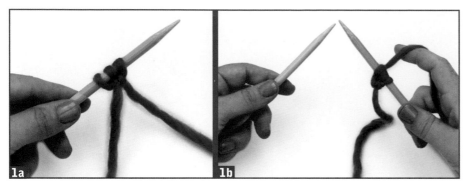

1. With a double-pointed or circular needle, cast on the required number of stitches (1a) and knit across the row (1b).

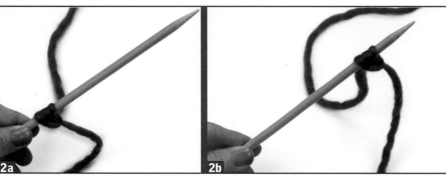

2. Do *not* turn work. Switch hands so that the needle with the stitches is in your left hand (2a).
Slide the stitches to the opposite end of the needle. The working yarn will appear to be at the wrong end of the row (2b).

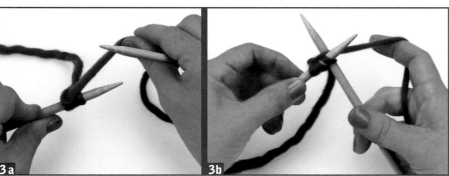

3. Bring the working yarn behind the stitches to the working end of needle, pulling it snugly (3a). Knit across the row. The strand of yarn stretched across the back will create a tube (3b).

4. Continue in this manner until your I-cord is the desired length. Bind off as you normally would.

■ KFB (KNIT FRONT & BACK)

This is a great increase to use with garter stitch because the bump created by this method gets hidden within the ridge pattern.

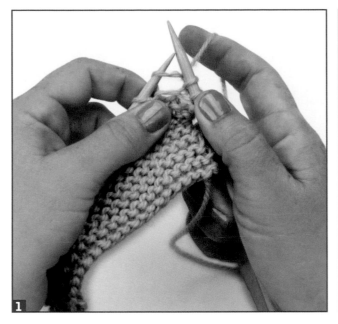

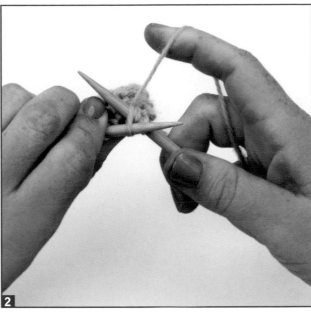

1. Knit into the front loop of stitch as normal *without* dropping stitch off the left-hand needle.

2. Knit into the back loop of the same stitch.

3. Let stitch drop off left-hand needle. One stitch has been increased.

■ SK2P

There are many ways to decrease stitches, some more complicated than others. SK2P is a quick and easy method to decrease two stitches at once.

1. Slip the next stitch knitwise onto the right-hand needle.

2. Knit the next two stitches together.

3. Insert the left-hand needle into the slipped stitch (3a). Pull the slipped stitch over the stitches you knit together and drop it off the needle (3b). Two stitches have been decreased.

■ WRAP & TURN (FOR GARTER STITCH SHORT-ROWS)

My favorite thing about working short rows in garter stitch is that the wrapped stitches don't need to be dealt with. They hide themselves amongst the garter bumps when you knit back over them!

1. Slip the next stitch needle purlwise.

2. Bring the yarn forward.

3. Return the slipped stitch back to the left-hand needle.

4. Turn your work. The stitch you slipped is now wrapped. You will now be on the wrong side of the work and will knit to the end of the row without having worked the stitches on the other side of the wrapped stitch.

■ 6-ST SL ST LC

Cables are one of the most iconic techniques in knitting. Once you learn the basics, it's fun to experiment with little cable variations—like this one!

1. Slip 3 stitches to a cable needle (1a). Hold these stitches in the front of your work (1b).

2. Working from the left-hand needle, knit 2 stitches (2a) and then slip 1 stitch (2b).

3. Working from the cable needle, slip 1 stitch (3a) and then knit 2 stitches (3b).

Binding Off

■ BASIC BIND-OFF

This is your classic, go-to bind-off method.

1. Knit two stitches.

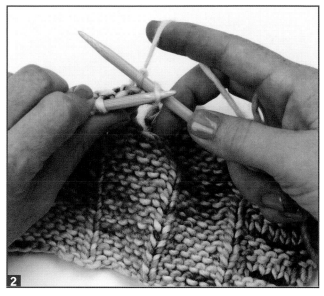

2. *Slip the tip of the left-hand needle into the second stitch on the right-hand needle (the one furthest to the right).

3. Pull the stitch over the first and off the needle. You'll now have only one stitch on the right-hand needle.

4. Knit the next stitch and repeat from * until only one stitch remains on both needles. Break off the yarn, and fasten off this stitch.

■ GARTER KITCHENER STITCH

This is a seaming method for grafting two garter-stitch pieces together. It creates a nearly seamless join—and it's easier to remember than the traditional Kitchener stitch method. Since you will use the yarn tail for this seaming method, make sure to cut the tail at least twice the length of the seam to give yourself enough yarn to work with.

1. Place stitches on two needles with back stitches showing a knit row, and front stitches showing a purl "bump" row.

2. Front needle: Insert tapestry needle *purlwise* into the first stitch; pull the yarn through, but leave the stitch on needle

3. Back needle: Insert tapestry needle *purlwise* into the first stitch; pull the yarn through, but leave the stitch on needle.

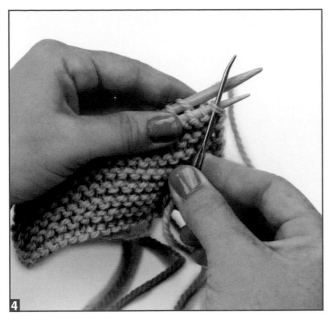

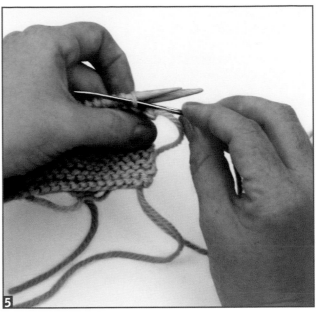

4. *Front needle: Insert tapestry needle *knitwise* into first stitch, letting it slip off the knitting needle as you pull the yarn through.

5. Front needle: Insert tapestry needle *purlwise* into current first stitch, but do *not* let it slip off as you pull the yarn through.

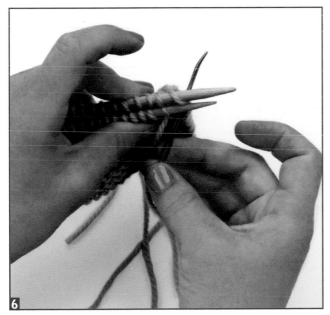

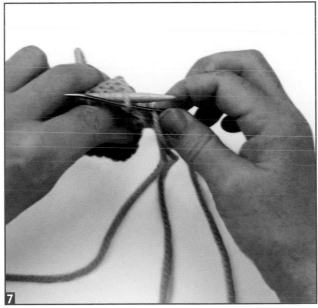

6. Back needle: Insert tapestry needle *knitwise* into first stitch, letting it slip off the knitting needle as you pull the yarn through.

7. Back needle: Insert the tapestry needle *purlwise* into current first stitch, but do *not* let it slip off as you pull the yarn through.

Repeat from * until all stitches are grafted, and fasten off. To remember which direction to insert the tapestry needle, it helps to think "knit 1, purl 1" for each needle.

■ 3-NEEDLE BIND-OFF

Create extra-strong seaming for two knitted pieces (or one folded piece) with "live" stitches using this method. Hold the pieces with the right sides facing each other to hide the seam, or hold the pieces with the wrong sides facing each other for a decorative seam! Another great thing about this bind-off is that it has knitted and purled versions. For the knitted version, knit all stitches. For the purled version, purl all stitches.

1. With the two sets of lives stitches held together, insert a third needle knitwise (purlwise) through each of the first stitches.

2. Pull the working yarn through *both* stitches and slip *both* stitches off the left-hand needles to create *one* new stitch on the right-hand needle.

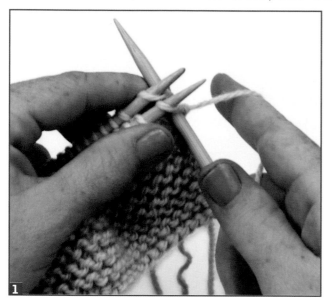

4. Slip the tip of a left-hand needle into the second stitch on the right-hand needle (the one furthest to the right). *(see page 87, Basic Bind Off, Step 2 photo)*

5. Pull the stitch over the first and off the needle. You'll now have only one stitch on the right-hand needle. *(see page 87, Basic Bind Off, Step 3 photo)*

6. Repeat from * until only one stitch remains and fasten off.

3. *Repeat steps 1 and 2 until two stitches are on the right-hand needle.

◆ Finishing

■ DUPLICATE STITCH ON GARTER

Traditionally, the duplicate stitch is used to "duplicate" the look of stockinette stitch. When used on garter, however it doesn't mock the bumps of the stitch so instead is used as a decorative, embroidered touch like the eyes of the motif on the Coyote Kid Sweater (see pages 71–75).

1. Using tapestry needle and yarn, come up through the base (the bottom of the V) of a knit stitch.

2. Come up and over the garter ridge (created by two knit rows), and dip behind the two loops of the knit stitch above. Pull the yarn through.

3. Go back down through the point of the V where you began (3a). One duplicate stitch is complete (3b).

■ SINGLE CROCHET EDGING (SC)

Sometimes crochet is the easiest and most effective way to add a stable edging to a knit piece. It's also especially useful if you want to wrap stitches around something like floral wire (see Birthday Baby Crowns, pages 44–45). Here's how to work the single crochet stitch when adding it to a knitted edge.

1. Tie a slipknot onto the crochet hook. Insert the hook into the front loop of the knitted edge stitch. You now have two loops (stitches) on your hook.

2. Wrap yarn counter-clockwise around the hook and draw it through the first loop.

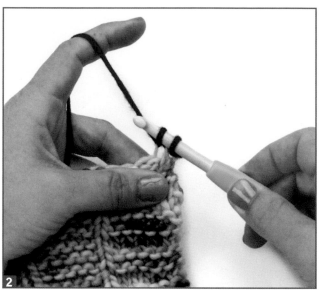

3. Wrap yarn once counter-clockwise again, and draw through both loops.

4. *Insert hook into the next knit stitch. Wrap yarn and draw through the first loop. Wrap yarn again and draw it through both loops. Continue from * until the edging is complete. Cut yarn and pull end through remaining loop.

Things to Know

ABBREVIATIONS

approx	approximately	**pfb**	purl into front and back of a stitch—one stitch has been increased	**spp**	slip, purl, pass sl st over
beg	begin(ning)			**ssk (ssp)**	slip 2 sts knitwise one at a time, insert LH needle through fronts of sts and knit (purl) together
CC	contrasting color				
ch	chain	**pat(s)**	pattern(s)		
cm	centimeter(s)	**pm**	place marker		
cn	cable needle	**psso**	pass slip stitch(es) over		
cont	continu(e)(ing)				
dec	decreas(e)(ing)	**p2tog**	purl two stitches together—one stitch has been decreased	**sssk**	slip 3 sts one at a time knitwise, insert LH needle through fronts of sts and knit together
dpn(s)	double-pointed needle(s)				
foll	follow(s)(ing)				
g	gram(s)	**rem**	remain(s)(ing)		
inc	increas(e)(ing)	**rep**	repeat	**st(s)**	stitch(es)
k	knit	**RH**	right-hand	**St st**	stockinette stitch
kfb	knit into the front and back of a stitch—one stitch has been increased	**RS**	right side(s)	**tbl**	through back loop(s)
		rnd(s)	round(s)	**tog**	together
		SKP	slip 1, knit 1, pass slip stitch over—one stitch has been decreased	**WS**	wrong side(s)
				wyib	with yarn in back
k2tog	knit 2 stitches together—one stitch has been decreased			**wyif**	with yarn in front
				yd(s)	yd(s)
		SK2P	slip 1, knit 2 together, pass slip stitch over the k2tog—two stitches decreased	**yo**	yarn over needle
LH	left-hand			*****	repeat directions following * as indicated
lp(s)	loop(s)				
m	meter(s)				
mm	millimeter(s)			**[ ]**	repeat directions inside brackets as indicated
MC	main color	**S2KP**	slip 2 stitches together, knit 1, pass 2 slip stitches over knit 1—two stitches decreased		
M1 or M1L	make one or make one left				
M1 p-st	make one purl stitch				
M1R	make one right	**sc**	single crochet		
oz	ounce(s)	**sl**	slip		
p	purl	**sl st**	slip stitch		

GAUGE

■ Make a test swatch at least 4"/10cm square. If the number of stitches and rows does not correspond to the gauge given, you must change the needle size. An easy rule to follow is: To get fewer stitches to the inch/cm, use a larger needle; to get more stitches to the inch/cm, use a smaller needle. Continue to try different needle sizes until you get the same number of stitches in the gauge.

SKILL LEVELS

◖◻◻◻
BEGINNER
Ideal first project.

◖◼◻◻
EASY
Basic stitches, minimal shaping, and simple finishing.

◖◼◼◻
INTERMEDIATE
For knitters with some experience. More intricate stitches, shaping, and finishing.

◖◼◼◻
EXPERIENCED
For knitters able to work patterns with complicated shaping and finishing.

Standard Yarn Weight System

CATAGORIES OF YARN, GAUGE RANGES, AND RECOMMENDED NEEDLE AND HOOK SIZES

Yarn Weight Symbol & Category	0 Lace	1 Super Fine	2 Fine	3 Light	4 Medium	5 Bulky	6 Super Bulky	7 Jumbo
Type of Yarns in Category	Fingering 10-count crochet thread	Sock, Fingering, Baby	Sport, Baby	DK, Light Worsted	Worsted, Afghan, Aran	Chunky, Craft, Rug	Super Bulky, Roving	Jumbo, Roving
Knit Gauge Range* in Stockinette Stitch to 4 inches	33–40** sts	27–32 sts	23–26 sts	21–24 sts	16–20 sts	12–15 sts	7–11 sts	6 sts and fewer
Recommended Needle in Metric Size Range	1.5–2.25 mm	2.25—3.25 mm	3.25—3.75 mm	3.75—4.5 mm	4.5—5.5 mm	5.5—8 mm	8—12.75 mm	12.75 mm and larger
Recommended Needle U.S. Size Range	000–1	1 to 3	3 to 5	5 to 7	7 to 9	9 to 11	11 to 17	17 and larger
Crochet Gauge* Ranges in Single Crochet to 4 inch	32–42 double crochets**	21–32 sts	16–20 sts	12–17 sts	11–14 sts	8–11 sts	6–9 sts	5 sts and fewer
Recommended Hook in Metric Size Range	Steel*** 1.6–1.4 mm	2.25—3.5 mm	3.5—4.5 mm	4.5—5.5 mm	5.5—6.5 mm	6.5—9 mm	9—16 mm	16 mm and larger
Recommended Hook U.S. Size Range	Steel*** 6, 7, 8 Regular hook B–1	B–1 to E–4	E–4 to 7	7 to I–9	I–9 to K–10 1/2	K–10 1/2 to M–13	M–13 to Q	Q and larger

* Guidelines only: The above reflect the most commonly used gauges and needle or hook sizes for specific yarn categories.

** Lace weight yarns are usually knitted or crocheted on larger needles and hooks to create lacy, openwork patterns. Accordingly, a gauge range is difficult to determine. Always follow the gauge stated in your pattern.

*** Steel crochet hooks are sized differently from regular hooks—the higher the number, the smaller the hook, which is the reverse of regular hook sizing.

KNITTING NEEDLES

U.S.	METRIC
0	2MM
1	2.25MM
2	2.75MM
3	3.25MM
4	3.5MM
5	3.75MM
6	4MM
7	4.5MM
8	5MM
9	5.5MM
10	6MM
10 ½	6.5MM
11	8MM
13	9MM
15	10MM
17	12.75MM
19	15MM
35	19MM

■ METRIC CONVERSIONS

To convert from inches to centimeters, simply multiply by 2.54.

page 29

page 38

page 42

Index

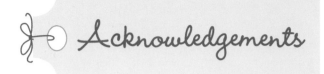

Acknowledgements

■ I've been working with the folks at Soho Publishing/Sixth&Spring Press in one way or another for the better part of a decade, but this is my first full-length book with them. Man, it's nice to work with people who know knitting! Even though whom I worked with changed during the production of *Wee Garter Stitch*, I never felt like my project wasn't a priority for the collective—thanks to the entire book department! My sincere appreciation also goes out to Laura Cooke, Lisa Silverman, and Jacob Seifert for their organization, communication, and encouragement; to Diane Lamphron for creating the cool, cute, and classic layout and design; to Carla Scott for her overall guidance; and to my friend, trusted mentor, colleague, and fellow Scorpio Trisha Malcolm for pushing, guiding, and straight-talking me through the realities of the craft-publishing world.

Many of the projects from this book wouldn't have made it from pattern draft to finished garments without the hard work of a few production stitchers: Chris Bahls, Leslie Tiras, Kim Neuhauser, and Libby Bailey (a.k.a Mom). Thank you!

My sincere appreciation goes out to Gayle Bunn for sharing her wealth of design knowledge whenever I had a question.

To Lori Steinberg, my longtime dear friend: I can't tell you how comforting it was to know that you'd be the one to whip my pattern drafts into book-ready shape. I appreciate all of your hard work!

To the MEOWer knitting group: I've been honored to have you in my life for my entire yarn-y career: your value is immeasurable. Thank you for being there during the ups, plateaus, and those SFD moments.

To our trainer, Britny, for babying my wrists and keeping my knitting arms strong, and my Pilates girls, Abeer, Chelsea & Jill, for making sure I take care of my body before I take care of business. Our bi-weekly sessions are like church for me.

To my closest buddies—Tammy, Sacha, Jennifer, Andee, and Kristin G.—and to my amazing network of friends: your shoulders and ears during the process of working on, finishing, and promoting back-to-back books over the past couple of years has kept me sane. Thank you for standing by me and having my back.

Lastly and most importantly, to my family, Dave, Tanner, Tristan, and Clover: thank you for loving me through the process of (yet again) piling too many things onto my overflowing work plate. Your faces give me perspective, and your hearts make everything worth it. I love you.

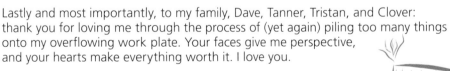

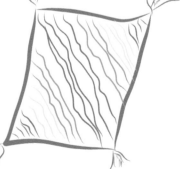